The Book of
Woolmer Green

A New Parish for the New Millennium

Compiled by the people of the parish

HALSGROVE

First published in Great Britain in 2001

*British Library Cataloguing-in-Publication Data
A CIP record for this title is available from the British Library*

ISBN 1 84114 1216

HALSGROVE
PUBLISHING, MEDIA AND DISTRIBUTION

*Halsgrove House
Lower Moor Way
Tiverton, Devon EX16 6SS
Tel: 01884 243242
Fax: 01884 243325
email: sales@halsgrove.com
website: http://www.halsgrove.com*

Frontispiece photograph: Hay tier outside the Red Lion c.1900 with the cart laden.

Printed and bound in Great Britain by Bookcraft Ltd, Midsomer Norton.

FOREWORD

I am honoured to be asked to contribute this foreword to *The Book of Woolmer Green*. The family connection with the village goes a long way back. Mardleybury and Paynes Farm were part of the Knebworth Estate until the post-war period. My great-grandmother, Edith, Countess of Lytton, laid the foundation stone of the Parish Church in September 1899. My own memories go back to shooting lunches in the Chequers Inn, skating on the pond at Mardleybury and, of course, countless journeys north and south along the Great North Road. Harry Macdonald's Woodcarver's Cottage was an important childhood landmark and I do not think that I am alone in deeply regretting its destruction.

I congratulate Woolmer Green on becoming a parish and offer my best wishes and those of my family for the new millennium.

David Lytton Cobbold
2ND LORD COBBOLD OF KNEBWORTH
AD2001

Bertha Groom (later Mrs Kaye), aged 17, milkmaid at Mardleybury Farm in the early 1900s.

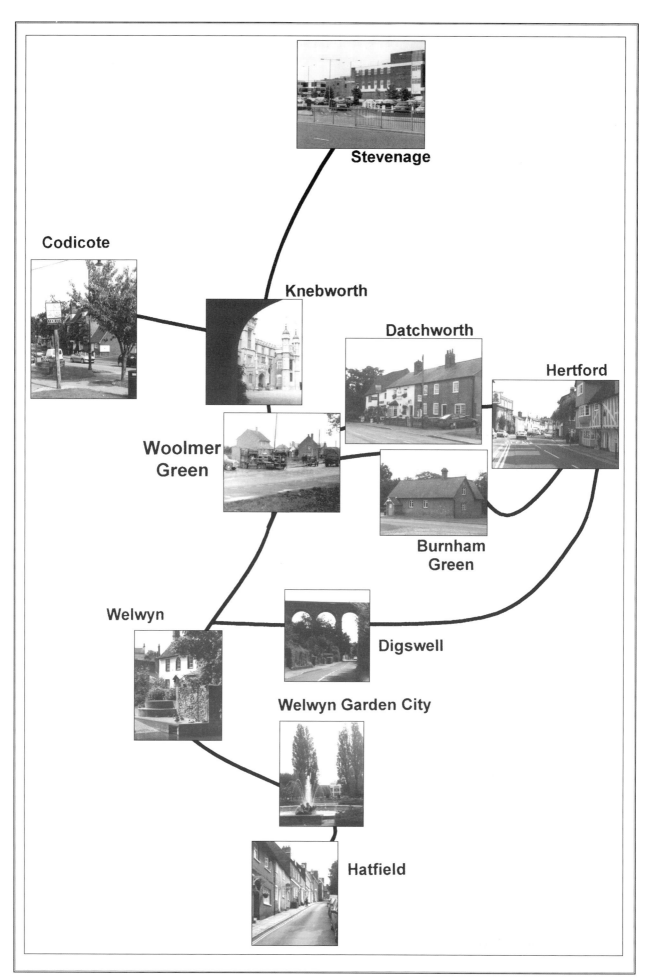

Stevenage

Codicote

Knebworth

Datchworth

Hertford

Woolmer
Green

Burnham
Green

Welwyn

Digswell

Welwyn Garden City

Hatfield

CONTENTS

A very early photograph of Woolmer Green Pond, New Road.

Acknowledgements

Thanks are due to the following bodies for their invaluable help in the compilation of this volume: Community Development Association, Hertfordshire; Community Media Ltd, formerly *North Herts Gazette*; Hertfordshire Archives and Local Studies for the pictures on pages 13, 44, 51, 52, 93, 97, 137 and 148; *Hertfordshire Countryside Magazine* and its contributors, in particular Frank E. Ballin and J.M. Stoddard; The Hertfordshire Society; David Hugill, photographer, Codicote; McMullens Brewery, Hertford; Kingsley Michael, photographers, Stevenage and Letchworth; Mill Green Museum, Welwyn Hatfield Council; *Welwyn and Hatfield Times* and its predecessors; Nigel Willoughby, photographer; the Church of St Michael's and All Angels, Woolmer Green; St Michael's School, Woolmer Green; Woolmer Green Carpet Bowls Club; Woolmer Green Nursery Group; Woolmer Green Rangers Football Club; Woolmer Green Women's Institute.

In addition the following individuals have all contributed in some way – large or small – to the success of the project: Enid Aitchison, Fred Archer, Terry Archer, the Ayres family, Chris Bazalgette, David Brownsell, the Buckle family, the Catlin family, Ian Chipperfield, John Collins, Daniel Cooke, Rosemary Cooper, Carol Cox, Geoff Cox, Ray Cox and Lisle's Garage, Mollie and Arthur Cummings and the Sequence Dance Club, Geoffrey and Susan Dash, Val and Eddie Deards, Doug Dietrich, Tuse Drury, Ted Elliott, Vena Evans, Enid Fairhead, Brenda and Bill Giddens, the Graves family, Nellie and Singh Grewal, Jeff Jackson, Tina and Nigel Jolly, Lucy Jordan, Barry Lake, Vera Mardlin, Eva Moody, Joy Nicholson, Pam Norris, Mrs O'Connel (Miss Powles), Eileen Orton, Ken Sisseman, Phyllis and Dick Smalley, Shirley Staniforth and the Brownies, David and Jane Thom, Doris Tyler, Nob and Vi Tyler, Paul Weatherhead, Jack and Margaret Webber, Jean and Peter Webber, and many others. The pen-and-ink drawings included in the book are by kind permission of Deborah Rehmat. Finally, acknowledgement should be made to E.J. Beard for the wonderfully helpful volume *Hamlet to Village: A Study of Woolmer Green 1840–1900*.

The Pond, Woolmer Green, early 1900s.

Judith Watson, Len Linnett, Betsy Linnett, David Watson and children of the village lay turf around the pond after its restoration in 1997.

Introduction

Woolmer Green has always been one of those places which is neither here nor there! In the Middle Ages part of the village was in Mardleybury Manor, part in Rectory Manor with the northern part owing allegiance to Broadwater Manor or Knebworth. Things have not changed; the village is still at the point where the Districts of North Herts, East Herts and Welwyn Hatfield meet. No wonder there is sometimes difficulty with our identity! In Roman times the village was at the junction of two thoroughfares, the Great North Road and another road called Stane Street which crossed this just south of the church, linking St Albans with Braughing and Colchester. Thomas de Wolvesmere is recorded as having lived in a dwelling here in 1297.

Apart from the trade generated by travellers, life in Woolmer Green was agricultural and feudal until the middle of the nineteenth century. Things started to change, however, when the railway arrived in 1850 (although the station in Knebworth was not opened until 1884 after intervention from Viscount Knebworth). The school, which was opened a few years after this, obtained much funding from the railway.

In 1863, only a gunsmith and a shoemaker were listed in the trade directory. By 1898, when the population of Woolmer Green stood at 363 and that of Knebworth at 382, there were five shops including two beer retailers; no mention in the trade directory of the many 'front room shops'! This level of service persisted until recent years with a general store and Post Office, a baker's, a small supermarket and a butcher's. Sadly, these have all now closed.

The main road through the centre of the village was still the Great North Road down which thousands of cattle and sheep were driven 'on the hoof' to London markets each year. The area around Knebworth and Woolmer Green provided what was probably the last overnight stop for the animals and their drovers before they reached London. Things sound good when looked at in retrospect but the majority of the residents of Woolmer Green were dependent on farming and the 1879 harvest was the worst of the century, resulting in many farms in the area not being let and thus labourers

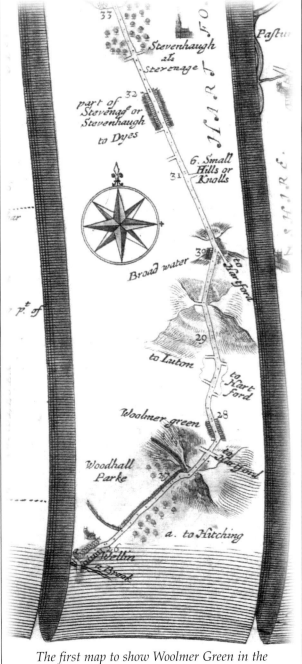

The first map to show Woolmer Green in the mid-18th century.

not being employed to work on them. At this time there was quite an influx of farmers from Scotland and Cornwall: they must have considered the prospects here to be better than their own!

In 1881, the Marquess of Salisbury installed electricity at Hatfield House where he had an internal telephone system and plate glass – obviously a newsworthy item!

Prior to 1894, the Parochial Church Councils looked after all the aspects of life in their parish but after this date Parish Councils took over the civil functions and left the Parochial Church Councils to look after Church affairs only. Woolmer Green Parish Council met for the very first time in May 2000.

Enter the Parish of Woolmer Green from the south and you see the village nestling round the curve of the main road. The railway bridge forms the boundary of Woolmer Green parish and Welwyn parish from which we split off in the millennium year. In fact, the railway forms the western boundary of the parish, from quite a long way south of the bridge and including the lovely viaduct at Robbery Bottom Lane until the outskirts of Knebworth to the north. To the east, the parish stretches almost to Datchworth and includes Mardleybury Farm and Manor and also a great part of Welches' Farm where the line of the parish boundary must have been fixed a very long time ago, it is so convoluted. When the bounds were beaten by the parishioners of St Mary's Church in Welwyn, it was noted that the parish boundary seemed to be marked by the many ancient oak trees which we see in the fields around us.

This book does not set out to be a comprehensive history of Woolmer Green – we will leave that until later – but is based on an idea by Caroline Evans and includes stories that were told to her about life in the village as people remembered it. We are very lucky that so many of the people in the village have lived here all their lives. They are a close-knit community, most related to each other, and must have found it quite difficult over the last few years, during which there has been such an increase in the population. We have tried to be as accurate as possible but are sure that some inaccuracies will have crept in to our book. Suffice it to say that assembling it has been fascinating and we hope that you will find it an engaging read too.

Oliver Kimpton's business had shops at Welwyn and Woolmer Green and also delivered bread to Datchworth, Tewin, Aston, Shephall, Bragbury, Broadwater, part of Stevenage, Burnham Green, Harmer Green, Digswell, parts of Welwyn Garden City, Welwyn, The Ayots, Woolmer Green, Mardley Hill and Oaklands. In addition deliveries were made to several factory canteens in Stevenage and Welwyn Garden City. Kimptons employed about a dozen people or more, including Margaret Webber, seen here, and Hilda English. Oliver Kimpton won a Gold Medal in about 1930 and a Bronze a year or two later at the Bakers' Exhibition. It was he who let the woodcarver use his barn, just across the road from the bakery, when he first came to the village looking for premises.

PART ONE
Approaching Woolmer Green
from the South

Harry Archer with son Terry outside Mayshade House, the home of Joe Cussans, in 1943.

Over the Bridge & into Woolmer Green

The sign for Woolmer Green is just south of the railway bridge; after which the recently built houses in the woodland of Oaklands and Mardley Heath are left behind and the character of the countryside changes. During the Second World War the Home Guard had their HQ in the woods near the railway where the Scout camp has more recently been held. Mardley Heath was used for training by the Army and the village was often full of soldiers during the war years. Their lorries were parked down Bridge Road. One resident recalled: 'The last flying bomb of the war fell in the sewage beds near Robbery Bottom Lane.'

The Scout camp in the woods to the south of the village.

Cubs and Scouts from all over the region enjoy camping in the beautiful woods.

The 4th Battalion Herts Regiment of the Home Guard in 1940. Left to right, back: Punch Croft, Arthur Warren, Cpl Bill Gates, Cpl Alf Scott, Cpl Fred Monk, Lance Cpl Ernie Ayres, Bernie Leggett; front: Sgt Stan Males, Lt Fish, Lt Eyre, Sgt Knowles, Cpl Percy Jeffery.

Railway Cottages, Weatherheads & Twin Foxes

On your left are the four railway cottages, much as they were built, with a wonderful view over the rolling Hertfordshire countryside towards Burnham Green. On a field south of the church, crop marks of a double-ditch feature can be seen, approximately 25 metres long, probably the remains of a former Roman road from Verulamium to Braughing and Colchester (AD50–410).

The land on which the new development of Twin Foxes stands was once cultivated as gardens or allotments by village people. It was then taken over by Innes & Co., who used it as a base for their extraction of gravel from Mardley Heath. They intended building a railway siding on the strip of land at the back of the recreation ground for the gravel trains. The road was particularly busy when Stevenage New Town was being built owing to all the gravel being taken from Mardley Heath to make concrete.

Railway Cottages as they are today.

Railway Cottages in the early 1900s.

Mrs Weatherhead being shown how one of the new earth-moving machines really works.

In 1962, the barn at Weatherheads was bricked in. Pam Norris remembers that during the war there were allotments here and that her Dad had two or three on which he grew vegetables and kept some chickens. In 1961 Weatherheads bought the land and sold agricultural machinery from the original barn which they enclosed to store equipment.

The Old Cottage

There were originally three cottages on the site of The Old Cottage shown in these two pictures. It is thought that the site was built for agricultural workers. The building and garden belonged to William John Blake of Danesbury who gave part of his land for the school (visible in the picture top right) in 1859. After his death in 1875, the cottages were sold in 1919 by R.W. Blake to Walter and Robert Wallace, dairy farmers of Knebworth, who at that time seem to have bought quite a lot of property around Woolmer Green; they came from Scotland when the harvest here failed in 1879. In 1935 the property was sold to Phyllis Joyce Baylis, still being described as three cottages, but around this time the main building was extended and modernised and the separate building was knocked down. The remaining cottage was further extended after the war and it was then purchased in 1978 by the present owners, Mr and Mrs Dash. In 1983 it was listed as a Building of Special Architectural or Historic Interest under the Town and Country Planning Act of 1971.

A view of the village taken in the 1950s from Heath Road bridge. The school can be seen middle right and the snow-covered field is where Twin Foxes stands today; prior to this (beginning in 1962) agricultural machines were sold here by Weatherheads.

St Michael's School Through the Years

Woolmer Green was very fortunate to have had a school for 30 years before the establishment of school boards in 1870. It was not until 1876 that Parliament made education compulsory for all children between the ages of five and fourteen, although even then, in rural areas, the youngsters were often excused from lessons to help in agricultural work, especially at harvest time.

In 1874 Miss Jayne Payne was given a farewell present by the people of Woolmer Green to mark the end of her 35 years as a schoolmistress, so we know there was a school in the village as far back as 1839. Jane was the daughter of a farmer, William Payne, whose farmhouse became a private residence many years ago, and it is probable that she used a room there as a schoolroom. Later in life she was a founder of the local Mothers' Meeting. She lived until she was 88 and is buried in the churchyard.

The first of the two school buildings at Woolmer Green was built in 1859 on land given by William John Blake, of Danesbury. In the previous year he had caused a trust deed to be drawn up conveying 'all that close or parcel of land called Chequers Meat, containing two roods or thereabouts situated near Woolmer Green in the Parish of Welwyn to the rector and churchwardens of the parish of Welwyn in the county of Hertford.' This parcel of land was 'bounded on the North by the Public House called the Chequers and the ground thereto belonging to Sir Edward Earle Lytton, Baronet, on the East by the Turnpike Road leading from Welwyn to Stevenage and on the South by a Cottage and Garden belonging to me the said William John Blake.'

When education became compulsory, all schoolmasters and mistresses were bound to keep a log-book, and all schools had to be inspected annually by a qualified inspector appointed by the board. The first inspector was Revd C.T. Robinson, and he reported that there was 'a very fair beginning in both discipline and instruction'. But he was not without criticism, noting that the arithmetic, was 'very backward'.

In 1901, the report for the mixed school included the comment: 'The discipline and instruction of this excellent school deserve the highest praise, and the progress made in all the subjects of instruction is most satisfactory.' Again, for the infants: 'The discipline is very praiseworthy, and the instruction is sound and careful, and the general efficiency of this division is decidedly good.'

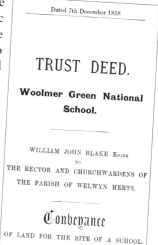

Dated 7th December 1858

TRUST DEED.

Woolmer Green National School.

WILLIAM JOHN BLAKE Esqre
TO
THE RECTOR AND CHURCHWARDENS OF THE PARISH OF WELWYN HERTS.

Conveyance

OF LAND FOR THE SITE OF A SCHOOL.

Woolmer Green School, c.1910. The schoolhouse had just been built.

WOOLMER GREEN SCHOOL.

YEAR ENDING 31ST MAY, 1899.

RECEIPTS.	£	s.	d.	PAYMENTS.	£	s.	d.
Balance from 1898	18	9	0½	Salaries	106	13	1
Government Grant	107	12	0	Fuel, Light, and Cleaning	17	19	6
Grant in aid	15	0	0	Books, Apparatus, etc.	21	15	6½
Subscriptions	23	12	0	Repairs	0	4	0
Private Individual Subscrip-				Rent	12	1	0
tion, G.N.R.	5	0	0	Insurance	1	5	0
				Sundries	1	18	7
				Balance	7	15	7
	£169	13	0½		£169	13	0½

LIST OF SUBSCRIBERS.

	£	s.	d.		£	s.	d.
A. M. Blake, Esq.	5	0	0	Miss Trower	5	0	0
Mrs. Blake	1	1	0	R. C. Vaughan, Esq.	1	0	0
N. S. Webb, Esq.	1	0	0	H. Pedder, Esq.	0	10	0
R. D. Balfour, Esq.	1	1	0	E. E. Bigge, Esq.	2	0	0
G. E. Dering, Esq.	3	0	0				
Rev. A. C. Headlam	2	0	0		£23	12	0
Lord Lytton	2	0	0				

Woolmer Green school accounts from 1899. In its early days the school was for the most part financed by a Government grant and by donations from the landowners of the district and the Great Northern Railway Co. Another source of income was 'school pence'. Each child was expected to bring 1d. to school every Monday as a contribution to their education. This was abolished in 1891, but the children were told they could still bring their money which would be paid into a boot club. When a child had enough in his/her account he or she was given an order to a local tradesman to buy a pair of boots or some other article of clothing which was required. There was also a 'coal and clothing' club in the village.

Dr Young's charity, 1899. It appears that the major funding for the building of the schoolhouse came from this charity. The charity was formed in Welwyn parish by a Dr Young and the trustees of his charity paid for the clothing and education of 16 boys at Welwyn who were chosen each year by the rector, and in 1887 they extended their munificence to Woolmer Green so that four boys and four girls could receive their schooling free, together with a distinctive dress.

DR. YOUNGS CHARITY.

ACCOUNT, 1899.

	£	s.	d.		£	s.	d.
Balance in hand	27	17	1	Lawrence, Apprentice Fee	10	0	0
Dividends	58	19	1	Welwyn Schools	25	0	0
Sale of Work	178	17	0	Clothing of Scholars	29	13	0
				Woolmer Green School House	200	0	0
				Balance in hand	1	0	2
	£265	13	2		£265	13	2

Charles Burgess and John Prior have been apprenticed. There will be no more funds for apprentice fees, for some little time.

DENNEY'S CHARITY.

ACCOUNT, 1899.

	£	s.	d.		£	s.	d.
Balance in hand	27	9	7	Mrs. Moulden	22	19	4
Dividends	22	19	4	Davis, Coal	10	10	0
				Balance	28	10	11
	£50	8	11		£50	8	11

DR. YOUNG'S SCHOLARS.

The following are the names of Dr. Young's Scholar's for 1899 :—

WELWYN.

William Prior.
Frank Adams.
Harry Davis.
Harry Philpott.
Frank Mairs.

William Dunn.
Amos Ilott.
Elijah Welch.
George Ellis.
Arthur Pateman.
Walter Mardell.

George Bennett.
George Ward.
James Bannister.
William Nash.
Herbert Hipgrave.

WOOLMER GREEN.

BOYS.
Percy Stratton.
Herbert Elsom.
Ernest Wisby.
Harry Dearmer.

GIRLS.
Laura Bennett.
Annie Sharp.
Laura Holton.
Ada Wrenn.

Dr Young's scholars at Woolmer Green School in 1899. Not on the list was the apparently popular teacher Miss Wood, who had left the school the previous year, as testified by a note which appeared in the Welwyn Parish Magazine in August 1898. Here we learn that Miss Wood was the lucky recipient of 'a very handsome desk' which was presented to her on her leaving her post as 'the teacher in the Infants' School at Woolmer Green'. Further note is made of the fact that: 'The money was entirely subscribed by the parents and children concerned with Woolmer Green School.'

Woolmer Green School, c.1900.

Schoolchildren at Woolmer Green in the early 1900s.

In the early days of the school, the nearest churches to Woolmer Green were St Mary's at Welwyn and All Saints', Datchworth. The long walk to services along the primitive roads of the period could not have been very pleasant in bad weather, so the villagers must have been extremely pleased when in 1878 'the wall which divided off the classroom at the end of the school was pierced with an arch and the room at the end fitted up as a chancel'. This was dedicated by the rector, the Revd Charles Lee Wingfield, and services were held here until St Michael's Church was built in 1900. That the weather was a bar to activities is demonstrated by the fact that in January 1899, on the afternoon of New Year's Day, there was a children's carol service at 3 o'clock, in St Mary's Hall, Welwyn. This was 'for all children, both of Welwyn and (if the weather allows) of Woolmer Green.'

From time to time additions had to be made to the school to cope with the increasing population, as until 1911, when a school was built at Knebworth, it had to cater for the educational needs of that village as well as those of several surrounding hamlets.

Until 1898 Woolmer Green had always been a 'dame's school,' but then it was decided that there should be a joint headmastership of husband and wife. This arrangement was in force until 1927, when Mr and Mrs Stacey retired after a joint headship which had lasted for 23 years.

The *Parish Magazine* for October 1901 contains the following entry under the heading which records 'School Attendances':

In 1900 there was an Act passed raising the age up to which children must attend School, and the Local Attendance Committee have now issued their new bye-laws. Attention is drawn to them as they are of great importance. The main rule is that every child between Five and Fourteen must attend school whenever school is opened, unless prevented by a reasonable excuse.

The following exemptions are allowed:-

1. If a child has passed the examination for the Fifth Standard, conducted by the Inspector, it is exempt from attending after Twelve.
2. A child over Twelve may become a half-timer, if in the same year it has passed the Fourth Standard, or if it has attended 300 times each year for five years.
3. Under the same conditions a child over Twelve may be exempt from school attendance between June 21st and October 21st if it has attended 250 times during the period from October 21st to June 21st preceding.
4. If a child over Eleven has passed the Fourth Standard, and has attended 250 times between October 21st to June 21st, it may be exempt from school until the following October 21st, for

employment in Agriculture. Such a child must in any case continue at school until it is Thirteen, even if it has passed the Fifth Standard.

It must be noted that it is not enough for a child to be in a certain standard at school, it must have gone in for and passed the examination conducted by the Inspector, and have received a certificate of exemption from the School Attendance Committee.

5. The attention of employers of labour as well as of parents is called to these rules.

The present schoolmaster's house, which is between the school and the Chequers, was built in 1903, and this was a great boon for all concerned, as previously some of the headteachers had to live at a fair distance from the school. From that time the schoolmaster acted also as choirmaster at St Michael's Church and Mr Stacey was also the churchwarden and treasurer.

One former pupil recalled: 'The road was quiet when I went to school, I could whip a top from the top of Mardley Hill all the way to school as there were only horses and carts.' Another memory was of 'a muffin man and the man with a bear on a chain'. The Flower Show, also clearly remembered, was held on the last Saturday of July, in the meadow opposite the church. 'The whole village took part and there was great competition among one and all.' Mr Stacey, the headmaster, was the chief organiser of this event, which also included sport.

One person recalled that the school was 'only the front building, in which were three classes', and that the toilets were outside. Games played were 'hopscotch, skipping, tag and marbles'. School meals were served in the Village Hall so at midday the children were all crossed over the road to the hall for dinner. They also had a bottle of milk mid-morning.

Once a year was the school's sports day against other schools at Tewin and Datchworth. Wednesday afternoons were particularly memorable in 1942 when 'there was gardening at the back of the school in a big plot where the headmaster was in control. In the afternoon there was perhaps a nature walk through the wood.' Gardening was a real novelty for the London evacuees who swelled numbers and there were two brothers who were most upset when their parents took them home. Sadly they were both killed in a raid. ('There wasn't much fighting between the village kids and the evacuees, more a friendly rivalry.')

The school day was characterised by a more formal timetable in the morning than in the afternoon, but whatever the subject, 'the classroom was cramped, screened from the infants there was little chance for creating displays'.

Mr Whittington, who lived in the schoolhouse, is remembered as 'an absolutely marvellous man' who could sort out any trouble.

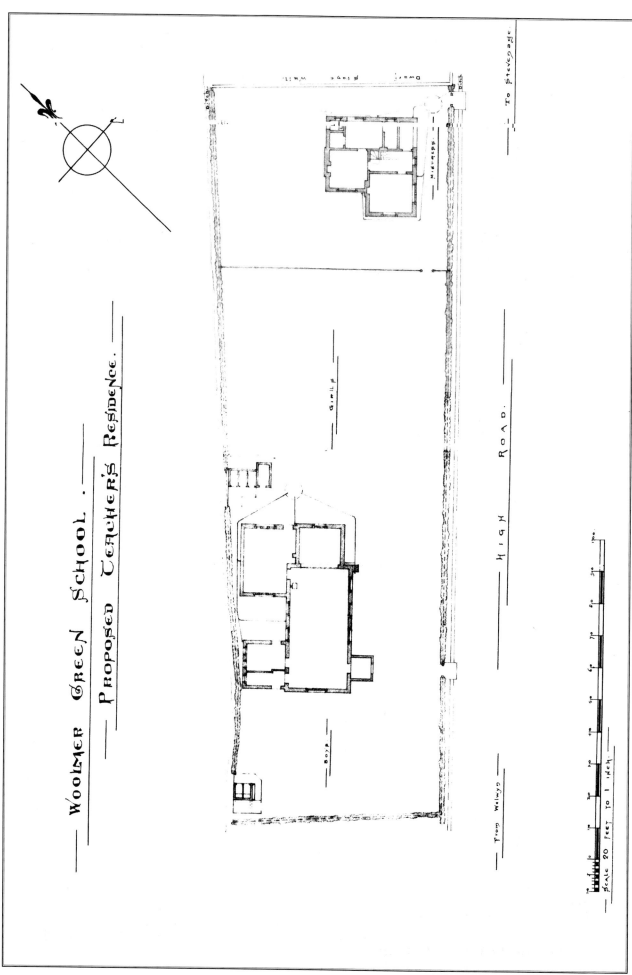

WOOLMER GREEN SCHOOL.

— PROPOSED TEACHER'S RESIDENCE. —

SCALE 20 FEET TO 1 INCH.

HIGH ROAD.

To Stevenage.

From Welwyn

Boys

Girls

Mistress

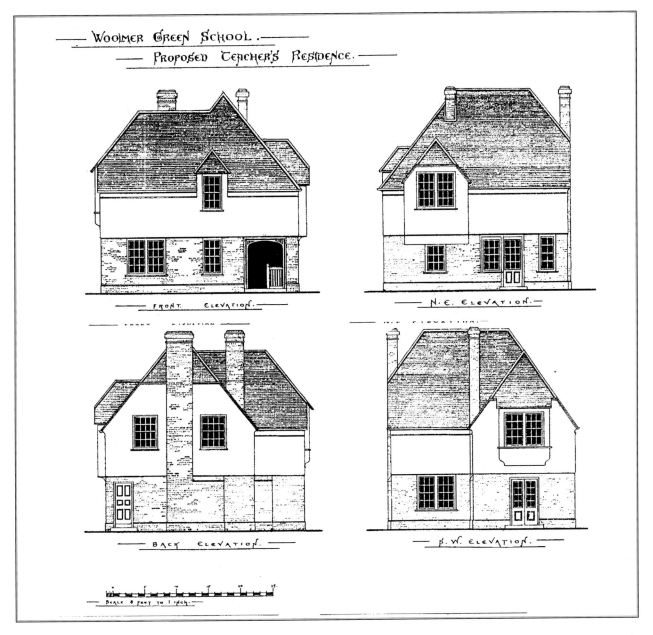

WOOLMER GREEN SCHOOL.
PROPOSED TEACHER'S RESIDENCE.

FRONT ELEVATION.

N.E. ELEVATION.

BACK ELEVATION.

S.W. ELEVATION.

SCALE 8 FEET TO 1 INCH.

The architect's plans showing the outside of the property from all four elevations.

The architect's drawings for the new schoolhouse were approved by 'EDUCATION' on 24 August 1898. The schoolhouse is for the most part unchanged to this day with fireplaces still in the main two rooms. Presumably one of the small rooms at the back was a wash-house and the other a coal-house; but note the drain from the sink running into the ditch along the back of the school! The boys and girls had their own separate playgrounds with an outside lavatory block; each looks as though it drains into a soakaway at the back of the block. Where would the toilet for the teacher have been?

A sampler worked by Annie Pedder at the school in 1913.

ABCDEFGHIJKLMN
OPQRSTUVWXYZ
abcdefghijklmnopqrstu
wxyz

Remember now thy Creator
in the days of thy youth —
1234567 Annie Pedder
890 Woolmer Green
1913

The decorated pram competition on the occasion of the coronation in 1937.
Pam Norris is wheeling the pram on the right of the picture.

Woolmer Green School in 1937. Left to right, back: Peggy Welch, Pat Beales, N. Chapman, Irene Warren,
Freddy Day, Freddy Tucker, Les Gregory, Audrey Timms, Millie Pratt, Hazel Warren;
4th row: Roy Edwards, June Eaton, Alan Cracknel, Kath Dearman, John Cotton, John Harridence,
May Davis, Donnie Sales, John Collins;
3rd row: Eileen Archer, Derek Gregory, Peggy Slater, Ernie Pettit, Gladys Burge, John Oakman,
Phyllis Harris, Arthur Randall, Betty Larman, Joan Harris, Tuse Bennett;
2nd row: ? Mitchell, Petal Carter, Billy Welch, Mary Davis, Dilly Slater, Donny Welch, Timmy Carter,
June Hipgrave, Kathy Buckle, Bobby Mitchell, Jean Snow;
front: Josie Clements, Audrey Beales, John Davis, Ben Harridence, ? Mason, Tuse Tucker,
Alan Grey, Daphne Harris, Derek Southall, J. Hipgrave.

School group, 1962. Left to right, back: Mr Mortemore, Nigel Deards, Adrian ?, Jason Hill, John Webber, Peter Long, Robin Skeggs; middle includes: Gillian Moss, Diane Sisseman, Martin Deards, Colin Gregory, John Smith, June Bowes, Linda Graves; front: Noreen Bennett, Mary Mortemore, Christine Mercer, Sue Graves, Julie Fletcher, Gillian Ayres. When the children played basketball or netball, Mr Mortemore stood with a wastepaper basket on his head as goal since the school did not have one!

Christine Orton and Howard Lawton at the school fête, c.1962. Money was still being raised for the school extension (which is the subject of the card in front).

School group, 1964. Left to right, back: Mrs Beard, John Blackman, Johnny Drury, Stuart Smith, Ivan Gregory, Martin Mercer, Andrew Overall; middle: Susan Morton, Helen Orton, Mary Monaghan, Jackie ?, Ann Mortemore, Christine Lawrence, Andrew Fletcher; front: ? Hancock, Eileen Jackson, Kathleen Monaghan, Helen Beck, Helen Buckle, Jill Nutting.

Mrs J. Beard leading Helen Orton on the pony at a school fête, c.1960s.

Marvin Norris and Ann Gregory receive prizes for winning a county-wide competition. Mr Clugston the headmaster is standing on the right.

The school fête in 1967: Leonard Parkin with Lorraine, Mandy, Trina and Marvin Norris.

Woolmer Green School Football Team, 1972/3. Left to right, back: Paul English, John Howell, Geoffrey Wakefield, Kevin Stammers, ?; front: Kevin Jeffries, Jonathan Bomfield, David Mills, Clark Clugston, Richard Snowden, John O'Shea, Raymond Slater, Stuart Figg.

125TH ANNIVERSARY

The 125 year celebrations with Leonie, Glenn, Angela, Sean, Stephen and Joanne.

ROLL OF HEADTEACHERS

1859   Jayne Payne
1875   Emily Carpenter
1878   Harriett Mary Hand
1879   Emma Baldwin
1890   Jessie Newham
1893   Emma Baldwin
1897   Edith Rose Pepper
1898   Robert & Harriett Goss
1899   George & Clara Turner
1904   Lampson & Emily Stacey
1927   Thomas Halliwell
1933   Alfred Richardson
1940   Albert Whittingham
1953   Henry Hodgkiss
1956   Norman Mortemore
1968   David Clugston
1976   Paul Stevens
1980   Brian Jolly
1992   Alison Witchell
1995   Tricia Ginsberg

A toll-gate was erected outside The Old Cottage.

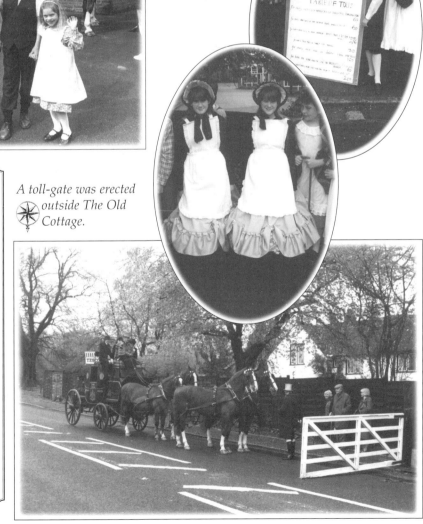

In June 1988 the school had its bell back after 50 years without one. Brian Jolly (headmaster), Terence Wenham (rector) and Pam Vincent (deputy head) are seen in the picture together with children from the school.

The girls' and boys' football team in 1993. Left to right, back row: Michael Dyson, Louise Neville, Cherry de Lacy, Edward Beattie, Richard Flynn, Malachy de Lacy; front: Rebecca Cunningham, Richard Saunders, Andrew Harris, Simon Lake, Robert Woods, Dean Hobbs, Luke Cracknell.

Woolmer Green Nursery occupies a room in the school and has been running for around 30 years. At one time, when there were more children than there are now, the nursery used the old school building. The numbers have dropped since the school started taking children a year earlier. In this photograph the children enjoy the Christmas play in 2000.

Schoolchildren, 2001.

School photograph in the millennium year.

CALENDAR FOR THE MONTH.

OBER.
Thursday. Matins, 8.40.
Friday. Matins, 8.40. Choir Practice, 7.45.
Saturday. Matins, 8.40. Woolmer Green—Coal and Clothing Clubs, 12.
Seventeenth Sunday after Trinity. Holy Communion, 8. Matins and Holy Communion, 11. Litany and Baptisms, 3. Evensong, 6. Hymns—M., 423, 321; E., 26, 222, 431. Woolmer Green—Matins, 11. Evensong, 6.
Monday. Matins, 8.40. Coal and Clothing Clubs, 12.
Tuesday. Woolmer Green—Choir Practice, 6.45.
Wednesday.
Thursday.
Friday. Choir Practice, 7.45.
Saturday. Woolmer Green—Coal and Clothing Clubs, 12.
Eighteenth Sunday after Trinity. WELWYN HARVEST FESTIVAL. Holy Communion, 8. Matins and Holy Communion, 11. Evensong, 6. Preacher—Rev. P. M. Wathen. Hymns—M., 378, 383, 382, 318, 316; E., 384, 386, 382, 601. Woolmer Green—Matins, 11; Litany and Baptisms, 3.15; Evensong, 6.
Monday. Coal and Clothing Clubs, 12.
Tuesday.
Wednesday. Woolmer Green—Choir Practice, 6.45.
Thursday. Woolmer Green Communicants' Guild, 7.
Friday. Choir Practice, 7.45.
Saturday. Woolmer Green—Coal and Clothing Clubs, 12.
Nineteenth Sunday after Trinity. Holy Communion, 8. Matins, 11. Evensong, 6. Hymns—M., 309, 433, 232; E., 13, 425, 235. WOOLMER GREEN HARVEST FESTIVAL. Holy Communion, 8; Matins and Holy Communion, 11; Children's Service, 3.15; Evensong, 6.
Monday. Coal and Clothing Clubs, 12.
Tuesday.
Wednesday. Woolmer Green—Choir Practice 6.45.
Thursday.
Friday. Choir Practice, 7.45.
Saturday. Woolmer Green—Coal and Clothing Clubs, 12.
Twentieth Sunday after Trinity. Holy Communion, 8. Matins, 11. Children's Service, 3. Evensong, 6. Hymns—M., 248, 517, 290. E., 193, 515, 228. Woolmer Green—Matins, 11; Evensong, 6.
Monday. Coal and Clothing Clubs, 12 (last day for paying in).
Tuesday.
Wednesday. SS. Simon and Jude. Holy Communion, 8. Matins, 12. Evensong, 6. Woolmer Green Choir Practice, 6.45.
Thursday.
Friday. Choir Practice, 7.45.
Saturday. Woolmer Green Coal and Clothing Clubs, 12 (last day for paying in).

NOVEMBER.
All Saints' Day. Twenty-First Sunday after Trinity. Holy Communion, 8. Matins and Holy Communion, 11. Litany and Baptisms, 3. Evensong, 6. Hymns—M., 436, 427, 426; E., 615, 428, 439, 437. Woolmer Green—Matins, 11; Evensong, 6.

PARISH REGISTER.

BAPTISMS.
August 30th. Jessie Ellen, daughter of Walter George and Edith Stagg.

AT WOOLMER GREEN.
Sept. 13th. William, son of William and Mary Jane Underwood.
" 16th. Gladys Inglett, daughter of Herbert John and Annie May Gooday.

MARRIAGE.
Sept. 12th. Charles John Arnold and Mary Ann Welch.

OFFICE

FOR

Laying the Foundation Stone

OF

The Church of St. Michael & All Angels,

At Woolmer Green,

IN THE PARISH OF WELWYN,

September 16th, 1899.

THE

FORM OF PRAYER

TO BE USED AT

The Consecration

OF THE

Chapel

and Burial Ground

OF

St. Michael and All Angels,

WOOLMER GREEN,

IN THE

PARISH OF WELWYN,

ON SATURDAY, NOV. 3RD, 1900, at 3 p.m.

BY

The Lord Bishop of St. Albans.

Sidesmen.
MR. TURNER.   MR. TAYLOR.

Clerk.
MR. E. CROFT.

Organists.
MRS. ANSELL.   MISS AMBROSE.

Sacristans.
MISS HIBBITT.   MRS. CHAPMAN.   MRS. CROFT.

Bell Ringer.
MRS. GAYLOR.

Choir.

MR. H. DEARMER.	MR. T. BENNETT.	MR. F. BEECHENER.
MR. L. DEARMER.	MR. SKEGGS.	MR. G. CARTER.
MR. C. BURGESS.	MR. J. BRYANS.	
FRANK KNAPP.	ERNEST WISBEY.	HERBERT SHARP.
HERBERT DEARMER.	FREDERICK DAVIS.	WILLIAM SKEGGS.
HERBERT ELSOM.	GEORGE DAVIS.	CHARLES AUSTIN.
PERCY STRATTON.	HARRY DEARMER.	DAVID BENNETT.
FRIEDA KNIGHT.	OLIVE SAUNDERS.	FLORRIE HARRADANCE.
AGNES BURGESS.	ETTIE COULDREY.	LILY CREASEY.
ROSE KNAPP.	BESSIE COULDREY.	ETTIE CREASEY.
ADA CHERRY.	NELLIE RIDING.	LAURA BENNETT.
LAURA HOLTON.	LILY WISBEY.	

Sunday School.
SUPERINTENDENT ... ... MISS HIBBITT.

Teachers.
MR. & MRS. TURNER.   MISSES F. KNIGHT, E. BURGESS, E. COULDREY.

The silver trowel used to lay the foundation stone.

One of the old grave markers in the churchyard of St Michael's.

The font

The Church & Cemetery

Though Sunday services had been held in the school since 1878 there were many people in Woolmer Green who thought it was high time that the village had its own church. This was a wish very dear to the heart of the Revd Edwin Hoskyns, who was a curate at Welwyn under Mr Wingfield when part of the school was consecrated as a church.

The following was reported in the *Welwyn Parish Magazine* in September 1898:

On Monday, August 29th, the two choirs of Welwyn and Woolmer Green went by Excursion train to Dover. The party numbered 74 in all; it started at 7 and was back at 12, after a fine and enjoyable day. Those who ventured by steamboat to the Goodwin Sands had a rather rough experience coming home. The Woolmer Green Choir owed their treat to the kindness of Mrs. Bigge.

The problem of finding a suitable site for the new church, which was to be dedicated to St Michael and All Angels, was soon solved when Lord Lytton presented the Church authorities with the plot of land at the junction of London Road and Mardleybury Road, which was to prove an ideal site with easy access for the majority of the villagers. The foundation stone was laid in September 1899 by Lady Lytton who used a silver trowel for the task.

It was suggested in the *Parish Magazine* in October 1899 that the children of the parish should contribute towards the cost of the font: 'Each can give very little, but the pennies and half-pennies of 350 children will quickly mount up, and all alike will feel they have a share in the new building.'

The church was to be named St Michael and All Angels in the hope that it would be consecrated at Michaelmas, 29 September 1900. However, it was not until 3 November 1900 that the consecration of the church and burial ground took place. The service was conducted by the Rt Revd John Festing, Bishop of St Albans:

The Bishop has appointed 3 o'clock on Saturday, November 3rd, for the consecration of the Church and Burial Ground at Woolmer Green. As the accommodation in the Church will be limited, tickets will be issued, which will be given in the first instance to those who have subscribed to, or collected for the Church, and to the inhabitants of Woolmer Green and Potters Heath.

The people of the village no longer needed to 'marry and bury' at Datchworth or Welwyn.

The porch was dedicated at Easter 1901 and in May: 'The Rector appointed Mr. R.C. Vaughan to act as his churchwarden at Woolmer Green, and Mr. J.T. Cross was elected people's warden.' Among the many benefactors of the new church we find the name of Colonel Arthur Maurice Blake of Danesbury whose uncle had given the land on which the school was to be built. Colonel Blake presented the porch and the contractor, Mr Lawrence, gave the front gates of the churchyard.

The choir consisted of eight men, eight boys and 14 girls (*see opposite page, centre right*).

The church was designed by Robert Weir Schultz (1860–1951), a modest example of late Arts and Crafts (it was said that the church design was suitable for the village of Woolmer Green!). The estimated cost was £2500 and the contract was given to Mr F. Lawrence of Datchworth. By October only £1500 had been promised so the decision was taken that only the walls and the roof of the church should be built, and the internal fittings left to be proceeded with as the money came in. It was originally felt that the church should have a tower but it proved impossible to raise the necessary funds (the drawings *top left and bottom* give a feel of what the church would have looked like had the tower been incorporated). The church screen is a significant example of late Arts-and-Crafts design and carving. It is said that the school bell was bought for the church in 1931 at a cost of £10.

Since the Revd R. Cattell was appointed there have been a total of 27 curates, living in various houses in the area until St Michael's House was built in the 1950s. Of many there are fond memories, like this comment which turned up about Father Leslie who 'involved the children and the village and organised the children on the hay wagon, which travelled around and blessed the crops.'

The church has generally remained sound, although in 1994 it became necessary to re-tile the roof, the money being raised mainly by public subscription and some grants. The churchyard has twice been extended and over 800 burials have taken place. The most recent extension will provide adequate space well into the future. St Michael's now looks forward to the next century. With it comes the need for further improvements to keep up with changing expectations. Fund-raising is still in hand for a toilet and extra accommodation in the vestry to house a range of activities.

The Rector's Watchful Eye

At the end of the nineteenth century, with the rector living in Welwyn, it must have been quite difficult to keep tabs on the church congregation. The houses in the village were drawn on a plan and their occupants identified, obviously by the then rector, Mr Ryder. Some of the families' histories are noted in great detail – particularly their antecedents – and whether they were dissenters, i.e. Nonconformists. On these two pages are a selection from Mr Ryder's notes and the note received from Mr Wilshere who supplied the same.

Dear Mr Walker

I came on these relics of the past the other day, and thought they might be of interest to you.

My sister received them from Mr Ryder – the then Rector – when we came here after my uncle's death. She will not want them now, I am sure.

Yr A Wils[...]

Paine Mrs, old widow – clean, deaf, respectable.
Miss Mary Paine – a great sufferer from cancer & spine complaint –
Miss Jane Paine – schoolmistress
Mary Ann Ibbets or (?) Hibbets niece of the above.

Haggar Mr & Mrs civil – she has fits (? epileptic) – a daughter of the Websters at Brascers End Lane 'The Fox'.

Hills Mr & Mrs old couple. He comes to church, – a little given to begging – she a regular imposter, – never comes to church because she cannot walk as far, but is often in at Welwyn. A grandchild lives with them – they have lodgers & the man employed by the Parish on the roads Name of lodger Bourke –

Bick Mr. & Mrs., 3 children –
works the telegraph at the Woolmer
Green hut. Very respectable –
regular attendants at Church.

Catlin Mr. & Mrs, dissenters – very
respectable – the village constable.

Pedder Mr & Mrs
son of old Pedder – not so steady
as the rest of the family –
never comes to Church

Saddler Mr & 2 sons – Church goers
one son not very steady.

Fletcher Mr & Mrs Shoemakers –
dissenters – respectable – employs
3 hands.

Kimpton Mr. & Mrs Carpenter – earns
good wages – 5 or 6 children –
pleasing but not very clean

Partly hidden by leaves but just visible is a carving of St Michael on the door.

Lime trees marking the boundary of the original churchyard.

✳ The names on the war memorial are as follows: 1914–18: Alfred Davis, William Dolby, Herbert Elsom, Thomas Holton, Albert Jackson, Alfred Jefferies, Richard Peddar, Arthur Sales, Ernest Sharp, Guy Vaughan, Arthur Waller; 1939–45: L. Bridger, H. Davis, E. Deards, J. Dobson, G. Parish, C. Penn, D. Penn, R. Sapsed, L. Scargill. Each year the British Legion attends on Remembrance Day and a service is held to honour the dead; wreaths are laid in their memory.

✳ Brian Leathers and Rob Slater discuss the best way to raise funds to re-tile the church roof.

The memorial window at the eastern end of ✳ the church is dedicated to the memory of Guy Carleton Vaughan of the Devonshire Regiment who was killed in action at Longueval on 20 July 1916 aged 26. He lived in the 'Cottage' now known as Mayshade and had only been married for a few months to his cousin Louise.

St Michael's Church Choir 1976–77. Left to right, back: Roger Beer, George Partridge (organist), Andrew Schunmann; 3rd row: Petra Schunmann, Elva Clark, Nicola Schunmann, Ethel Standing; 2nd row: Joanna Turk, Jane Nicolson, Father Leslie Gardner, Iris Gardner, Jane Lonergan; front: Kerry Schunmann, Beverley Gilbert, Janet Beer, Mark Smith, ?, Jackie Stevens, Nicola Gale, Julie Giddens, Damion Schunmann, Neil Smith.

The church noticeboard at the time of writing.

Dick and Phyllis Smalley, 1945. Phyllis' dress was bought on coupons, she had ATS borrowed shoes and a friend of her mother sewed some lace onto a plain ATS bra to make it pretty. The church was decorated with sheaves of corn as it was September and near Harvest Festival so it wasn't plain. Dick, her husband, was in his RAF uniform.

WOOLMER GREEN FLOWER SHOW AND SPORTS, FROM THE CHURCH MAGAZINE

On Saturday, July 26th [1901], the above took place in a field opposite Woolmer Green Church, kindly lent by Mr. S. Wallace. The exhibits were arranged in two tents kindly lent by A.M. Blake, Esq., and R.C. Vaughan. Esq. More than 250 exhibits were on view, all grown by residents in Woolmer Green. Mrs. Bigge, A.M. Blake, Esq., R.C. Vaughan, Esq., S.S. Berger, Esq. and M. Price, Esq. sent plants and roses to beautify the show. A very choice selection of roses was shown by R. Harkness and Son, Hitchin. About 400 people passed through the tents and stayed throughout the afternoon to witness the sports, which were carried on successfully under the direction of the Committee.

About 6 o'clock, during an interval, G.B. Hudson, Esq., M.P., distributed the prizes, and made a short speech to those assembled. A vote of thanks and cheers for Mr. Hudson, cheers for Mr. and Mrs. Vaughan, thanks to the judges, Messrs. Kipling, Sawford, and Fitt, and to Mr. Wallace concluded this part of the programme. The sports were then continued, the whole concluding with two exciting and sternly contested tugs-of-war; one between single and married of Woolmer Green, the latter gaining the victory, and the other between the representatives of Woolmer Green and a team of visitors, which was won by the former after a tremendous struggle.

Great credit is due to the two Honorary Secretaries, Mr. Stubbs, and Mr. Turner, who worked very hard to make the sports and flower show a success, and many thanks are due to Mr. Vaughan for his unfailing kindness.

The crucifix carved by the woodcarver of Woolmer Green, Harry Macdonald.

 Looking across at the Chequers from the garden of Swiss Cottage.

Chequers Corner is a common site for road accidents.

The Chequers

The Chequers probably started life as a wayside alehouse some time in the seventeenth century, but the present building dates from about 1927 when the Great North Road was widened. Certainly it was an alehouse in 1637 when Richard Nash was recorded as keeper. In 1719, John Blindell, who farmed Gun Farm at Knebworth, bequeathed his 'house called Chequers near Woolmer Green, now in the occupation of Abraham Venables' to his daughter Martha. The Chequers remained in Blindell hands for most of the century and in 1802 the licensee was Joseph Deller Gray.

During the nineteenth century the inn included a blacksmith's shop, a range of stabling and other buildings, and a pond in front with a water trough and signpost. It was bought by William Lucas, brewer, of Hitchin in 1818. In about 1800 the wife of the licensee, William Pelham, was sentenced to transportation for buying two silver spoons, knowing them to have been stolen (told by Ind Coope).

Chequers Corner where Mardleybury Road joins the London Road is infamous for accidents occurring when vehicles fail to negotiate the tight bend with the camber of the road in the wrong direction. 'You only had to go and sit on that corner and an accident was bound to happen!' was one comment received by the compilers of this volume. 'There was a military lorry didn't get round in the middle of the night and one of the men was knocked out and came to in the graveyard... must have been scary!'

The old Chequers Public House was demolished in 1927 when London Road was re-aligned to make it safer. Until that time the bend was a lot sharper and the camber even more in the wrong direction than it is now! Some of the kerbstones from the edge of the old road can still be seen in the footpath, giving some idea of how much the road surface was raised.

LOT 9.

The valuable Freehold Estate, situate at WOOLMER GREEN, Herts.,

(About 1 mile from the new Station, on the Great Northern Railway, at Knebworth, and 2 miles from WELWYN,) called or known as

"The Chequers," old licensed Public House,

Comprising the substantial brick-built and tiled DWELLING HOUSE,

Containing 2 front Bed-Rooms and Landing, 2 back Bed-Rooms, with 2 Staircases, Entrance-Passage and Private Door, Tap-Room, Parlour, small back Parlour, back Kitchen and Dairy, underground Cellar;

Large Front YARD with a brick and slated Blacksmith's Shop and Forge,

A Slated and Boarded Open Stable or Shoeing Shed adjoining; a Range of Boarded and Tiled Buildings, used as Stabling for six horses, a Boarded and Slated Chaise-House, W.C., and lean-to Coal or Wood House;

A LARGE ENCLOSED GARDEN in the rear

And Pond of Water in front; well situate with a frontage to the Street and Road leading to WELWYN; subject to a land tax of 17s. 6d. per annum.

The estimated Rent of this lot is £29 per annum.

Wat-er tipple for villagers!

REPORT BY JOHN ADAMS

● Beer will flow like pond water at the Chequers Inn

THIRSTY regulars at a village pub have a special treat in store for them this Bank Holiday weekend – pondwater.

And they will lap up gallons of the stuff. In fact, they are being challenged to drink the pond dry.

For this is not your common or garden pondwater, but a special beer. And the full proceeds from the sale of it will go towards restoring the pond in Woolmer Green.

It used to be the place where people would meet to talk, feed the ducks, or just sit by the water and reflect on life.

Silted up

But in recent years the pond has been neglected, become silted up and local people have stayed away from it.

Now the Woolmer Green Residents' Association want to put the pond back at the centre of village life.

That means draining it and removing the silt and debris. The cost of the operation is estimated to be a sobering £6,000.

Seeking ideas for raising the money, the association approached Steve Lathaen of the Chequers Inn, who threw down the challenge to get guzzling on the Pondwater.

To celebrate the sale of the brew on Easter Monday, the pub plans a full programme of entertainment for willing Pondwater drinkers.

It will include a ceilidh band, Irish dancing, juggling and magic. And there'll be a barbecue to tempt hungry patrons.

Steve thinks it will be a great day. He said: "Many people will want to relax and enjoy good food, drink and entertainment.

"If they can do this while raising money for the Woolmer Green Pond then that's fantastic.

"I would just like as many people as possible from the surrounding areas to come along and drink a few pints of Pondwater for a good cause. If we can raise all the money in a single day that would be great."

The lorry which ran into the house in 1958.

Son Collins outside his house in about 1950.

Son and Cis Collins at Swiss Cottage, 1958. Son was a hay tier who took local hay up to places in London where horses were kept, including the Barracks in Hyde Park and Buckingham Palace. Local farmers used to supply hay for railway horses at big London stations. Hay lorries from this area still supply the London Barracks to this day.

Swiss Cottage in 1988.

Son Collins chopping wood, c.1950.

After the demolition of Swiss Cottage, Mardleybury Court was built on the site.

Two modern views of Mayshade House.

Mayshade House, formerly 'The Cottage'

Next to Swiss Cottage stands another of Woolmer Green's listed buildings, Mayshade House, built in the eighteenth century. This was called The Cottage when Reginald Vaughan lived there before the church was built; he was the first churchwarden as well as one of the managers of Woolmer Green School. For many years he was a generous subscriber to church and village functions and was always ready to lend his spacious grounds for open-air fêtes. He must have been a colourful character and held 'long pipe' evenings when he invited villagers to entertainments at the school where the men were welcomed with a pipe, tobacco and beer to keep out the cold.

Mr Vaughan's daughter, Marie Louise, married her cousin, Captain Guy Carleton Vaughan, who was killed during the First World War. Three years later Mr Vaughan died suddenly; he is buried in the churchyard together with his wife and daughter.

The Cottage then came into the possession of Joseph Cussans, and many villagers still refer to the property by that name. Coal was delivered by Harry Archer using horse and cart during the war since petrol was strictly rationed.

Mr Cussans was well known for his work with old people and a room at Wellfield House in Hatfield is named after him. His first wife was one of the first presidents of Woolmer Green WI. After she died Mr Cussans had a bungalow built next to The Cottage where he lived when he married for the second time. He then sold The Cottage to Mr Dudley Morgan who changed the name of the house to Mayshade after the name of his wife's old home in Scotland. Mr Morgan was also a churchwarden for St Michael's and a school manager. He played a great part in the building of the new school and the consequent reorganisation of the foundation which during his time celebrated its centenary. Mrs Morgan was the Chairman of the Woolmer Green Branch of the Red Cross for several years.

The house was subsequently sold to its present owners Mr and Mrs Grewal; Mr Grewal carried on the tradition of previous owners for public service by acting as a Parish Councillor on Welwyn Parish Council for two years at the beginning of the 1990s. Some of the extensive grounds belonging to the property have now been sold off for development but the house itself looks much as it must have done many years ago.

The Woodcarver of Woolmer Green

A little further on and before reaching New Road was the woodcarver's barn and garden. There was a cottage here which had been lived in by Granny Cutts who was mid-wife to the village and later on there was a tea-room run by Enid Mokesam. In one of the cottages there was a physical training class held upstairs and later on there was a dancing class. Nob Tyler remembers the owner arriving home cross and throwing the wind-up gramophone out of the window because he couldn't stand the noise anymore.

There have been numerous articles written about woodcarver Harry Macdonald who set up his business in a barn belonging to Kimpton's, the bakers, at the junction of New Road and London Road.

His barn was covered with, and surrounded by, his wooden creations, from strangely shaped dogs to giant giraffes; from small, gaily-painted wooden figures to a huge reproduction of the children's poem 'The cow jumped over the moon'. The miniature village, composed of odd-shaped houses, 'Mac's Inn' and a church never failed to delight the children.

Harry's sculptures were magical.

It was quite by chance that Harry Macdonald came to Woolmer Green but his barn is remembered by all who used to travel down the Great North Road to London. It is widely acknowledged that Harry put Woolmer Green on the map.

He started out by making rustic garden furniture, but sales were few and spasmodic. To attract attention, he fashioned a giant figure of a policeman holding up an enormous hand. Never having done woodcarving before, the task was difficult, but his expert knowledge of the use of chisels proved that it was possible, and very soon afterwards the huge policeman made its appearance, calling upon all motorists to stop and buy!

From this first effort, the idea of woodcarving was born in Harry's mind. One of his early contracts was to carve a life-size stork for a maternity-home advertisement. He borrowed a model used to advertise a well-known brand of margarine, and, by doubling the size, eventually completed the giant bird. The customer's idea had been to hang a model baby from the stork's beak but Harry thought he would try the effect with a timber infant. He did not attempt to borrow a live model for this, however, but fashioned one according to his own ideas. The finished work occasioned a good deal of comment, some of it complimentary, some otherwise!

Harry still worked hard at carving models, but his greatest handicap was his utter ignorance of drawing and anatomy. To increase his knowledge he attended evening classes in art at St Albans, a round trip of 24 miles after his day's work. His efforts resulted in a contract to carve models for a leading firm of costumiers and large stores in London and other cities.

His work attracted the attention of several press agents who asked permission to take photographs and these duly appeared in a number of newspapers and periodicals including the *London Star*, the *Yorkshire Post*, *Sunday Dispatch* and even in an American journal from which came a commission from a place as far away as Indiana, USA.

During the Second World War Harry Macdonald was the air-raid warden for Woolmer Green and his work was often interrupted by air raids and other contingencies, such as in 1942 when a military lorry travelling at night (no lights allowed then remember) crashed into his premises and completely demolished his garden display. One of the men was asleep in the lorry, which turned two complete somersaults before coming to rest. When he came to his senses, finding one or two of Harry's life-sized models lying prone around him, he thought he was dead. During the conflict a number of visitors, including Americans and Australians, called on him and said they had recognized the exhibition from various films and magazines.

Harry's commissions have included a carved chest for an RAF memorial in a church, a baby Christ for a convent and three heraldic banners for Hill End Hospital Chapel, a crucifix for a parish church in South Africa and another for an Indian Church. Harry was commissioned by the Hertfordshire Society to carve the trophy for the best-kept village sign which is awarded annually. The press report for the event read as follows:

The carved village sign which is erected in the best-kept village of Hertfordshire, and which will be proudly displayed in High Wych this year, is representative of a craft of which the county can be justly proud. Mr. E.H. Doubleday, the County Planning Officer, said on Tuesday: "We are entering this sign in the Hertfordshire and District Chapter of Architects competition for the finest examples of craft work. It has been executed by Mr. Harry Macdonald the woodcarver of Woolmer Green."

Harry's cottage – a landmark for visitors and locals alike.

One of the first miniature villages in the country.

Harry at work in his studio.

Harry's Best Kept Village sign.

This is an extract from the article which appeared in the *Welwyn Times and Hatfield Advertiser*, 26 March 1973:

ANGRY VILLAGERS CLAIM COUNCILLORS SNUBBED THEM

... the Woodcarver's Cottage at Woolmer Green has little architectural merit and... the Council could not insist that 'only a woodcarver lived there.' Councillor Ray Little was speaking after visiting the site with members of Welwyn Hatfield Highways Committee. He said that the main objections the Council had received were concerned with the extra vehicles the proposed restaurant-tea room would attract.

He said a picture recently in the Times Advertiser showed a massive queue outside the cottage when it was open to the public. "Where did people park their cars and why didn't anyone complain then?" asked Cllr. Little.

He added that the people of Woolmer Green had to realise that the council could not insist that a woodcarver occupied the cottage. He said: "The house has very little architectural merit but the matter will be discussed by the full committee before a decision is taken."

Angry villagers turned out in force when councillors visited the site. But the councillors hardly talked to the demonstrators and some villagers thought they had been snubbed.

Mr. Frederick Wilcox from the local post office said: "This is a very dangerous corner and there have been a large number of accidents here. Apart from that there is little need for a restaurant round here, the pubs provide all that sort of thing."

Harry had been such a favourite with children (he is pictured here with Jane, Julia and Anthony Nicolson), and after he died there was the question of what to do with his life's work. Some people favoured making the house and grounds into a museum and others thought a tea shop there would be good. All too quickly, the site was sold to a developer and the house and garden bulldozed to make way for housing. The people in the village protested too little and too late.

Harry's brother was a missionary in Ovamboland and Harry raised funds for him in Woolmer Green. He is seen here with Mrs Kaye.

Harry creating a model church tower.

Woolmer Green Post Office in the 1970s. It was a sad day when the Post Office closed, for it had served as the meeting place for the whole village – 'Chris doing the Post Office bit knew everyone and everyone's children and the children used to draw pictures for her and she would put them up in the shop.'

You can still just see the painted sign on the side of the building advertising Pedder's Stores. It reads: 'W. Gates, Pedder's Store, Grocery, Provisions, Wine, etc., Cigarettes, Tobacco and Sweets all at Market Prices.

From the School Field to Kimptons & the Post Office

On the opposite side of the road is the school field where the house which was once the Police House stands. One of the policemen to live here was Chris Hoar, who like others in the service, was a regular feature of village life, often to be seen riding around on his bicycle. He knew everybody and everything that went on. Locals recall being caught out by PC Hoar for a variety of misdemeanours: 'He saw me crossing the road where I shouldn't and came up to the house and told my mum and I got a smack', and 'He caught us with two rabbits that we'd poached... "What's that you've got there? I'll take one of those off you!"'

The school was originally only the old building and the immediate surroundings and the field was acquired later. The field was the site of many celebrations. On 7 June 1977 locals celebrated the Queen's silver jubilee. Among recollections of the events are these three accounts: 'We had a party in the school field and the children had tea and fancy dress, dressed as kings and queens...'; 'The children were each given a jubilee certificate and flag. There were races and Gary won a mug and jubilee notebook...'; and 'There was a disco dance and ploughmans in the evening and everybody enjoyed themselves.' Now only a small piece of the school field has a frontage on to the London Road.

Crossing New Road, which used to be called Braggers End Lane, is a shop with a pillar box outside.

This was the Post Office and general store until 1997. Ever since the road layout at this point was changed it has been exceedingly difficult to get out of New Road because of the cars in the layby. There have been petitions, complaints, etc. but as yet no change.

Facing the Post Office was Kimptons, the bakery and general store. Oliver Bentley Kimpton (1890–1958) lived at Weston near Stevenage when he was young. He joined the Navy as a baker in the First World War and left in early 1920, after which he set up business in Woolmer Green. He never married but employed a housekeeper, Miss Kubler. On his death on 24 August 1958, aged 68, he left his business and property to Miss Kubler. It was then run as a company until 1973 (when the housekeeper died) by three key workers: Mr L. Rumbles (Manager), Mr H. Ferguson (confectioner) and Mr J. Webber (baker and supervisor, of New Road). When Miss Kubler died, she left the concern to two of her sisters. Having no interest in baking they sold the bakehouse and shop to Pearce Bakeries of Stevenage. All the staff were made redundant and the rounds given up, deliveries having been made to all of the big houses in the area. After a few years Pearce Bakeries moved their operations to Hertford and the old bakehouse was sold to Nigel Jones, asbestos removers. They altered the premises to suit their needs removing all the ovens, etc. and letting the shop to Tony Kan as a Chinese Takeaway.

Kimptons

I wrote a letter to Kimptons shop. The first owner of the shop was called Oliver Kimpton. The shop was made in about 1860. The brick bond is the Flemis bond. Kimptons is next to the Video shop and the butchers.

On the chimney they have three Television aerials. The shop is big and white. Kimptons is a kind of Small supermarket. It is also set back from the pavement so that cars can park there.

Brian Jolly, headmaster of Woolmer Green School, organised a Domesday Book survey by Year 5–6 of some of the houses in the village in 1988/89. These accounts from the schoolchildren plus Brian's pictures are interspersed throughout the book.

PART TWO
Approaching Woolmer Green from the West

Coronation party, 1953, on the green in front of the pre-fabs.
Included are: the Beck children, Nigel and Martyn Deards in the twin pram,
Pat Aldridge, Mr and Mrs Pettit, Ann Leggett, Michael Groom,
Tony Manning, Malcolm Deards, Roy Stammers.

The Railway

Entering the village from the west, one arrives via Wych Elm Lane where the children used to go up to the Iron House. Wooden, with a corrugated iron roof, the building was out of bounds to children, especially the girls. Tramps and itinerant workers would stay there, often with a bottle of the strong stuff for company. It was a favourite dare for village boys to creep up to the window and peer in.

The nearby railway line marks the western boundary of the parish. The small viaduct to the south, at the end of Robbery Bottom Lane (*below*), follows the same design as the long viaduct at Digswell. It was designed by William Cubitt and built by Thomas Brassey between 1848 and 1850.

An additional bridge will probably be built to the east if the East Coast Main Line widening takes place. The bridge over London Road and that over Heath Road will then be replaced. All three of these structures are original, dating from when the railway was first built, although they have been strengthened and the parapets raised.

There used to be a halt at Woolmer Green during the war which was used by soldiers. Nowadays, our nearest station is at Knebworth. Mr Cross, who used to live at 2, New Road, was the Stationmaster at Knebworth, a very important gentleman.

The Parliamentary Bill for the London to York Railway was passed in 1846 and in 1847, 8000 navvies were set to work on the line which passed through Woolmer Green. In 1850 Queen Victoria made the opening ride on the railway. It's amazing how quickly things were done then!

The station in Knebworth was not built until 1884, at the request of Viscount Knebworth, and until then the railway was used as a means of transferring manure from all the stables in London to a convenient place in the country. Chutes were constructed so that the manure could be shovelled down on to the roads and the local farmers then picked it up to use as fertiliser.

There was a signal box near the bridge in Bridge Road which was at one time manned by Peter Burgess. The line at this time was a single track and trains coming down to London would have to wait before going through to Welwyn. According to William Fletcher, when they reached the signal box at Woolmer Green they apparently halted and if there was a delay, the crew left their train and walked across to the Red Lion for a drink. When the line was clear Peter Burgess would give them a shout and back they would come to continue their journey.

A steam train crossing the viaduct at Robbery Bottom Lane.

A diesel train emerging from the tunnel just south of the London Road Bridge.

The Silver Link, about to go under Heath Road Bridge, 1937.

London Road Bridge.

This view of the railway line in the 1950s shows Weatherheads agricultural machinery business on the right.

This was the first diesel train to run on the line, 1957.

LIVING NEAR THE RAILWAY

Living by the railway had many disadvantages, not least the fact that one's clothes often got smutty whilst hanging on the line to dry. But it also had its advantages, as testified by one erstwhile railway-side resident:

I went along the side of the railway near the woods with my little boy, looking for coal and a slow train came along and the driver and fireman kicked out two great big lumps of coal, which rolled down the bank from the train. We carried it home and put it in the coal shed and I couldn't wait to tell my husband who could hardly believe it when we showed him the shed full of coal.

After the railway bridge is a street of houses most of which were built by the Rural District Council between the wars. Before these were rendered you could see the bullet holes in the walls caused by enemy planes flying up the railway.

'COMMUTING FROM LONDON TO WOOLMER GREEN BY RAIL IN THE RUSH HOUR'
by Enid Fairhead

Shoved and pushed
Pushed and shoved
Squeezed and squashed
Squashed and pinned
Sliding doors
Seal us in
Relentlessly

NO AIR

Coughing, spluttering
Sniffing, blowing…
Rib to Rib, lungs are cramped
Elbows, knees, feet are clamped…
Finsbury Park left behind
You are on my foot – do you mind!

Concrete blank, chimneys black

Bricks and mortar, stack on stack
Chinks of grey, squints of brown
Nameless stations flashing past
And – at – last –

Between the hats and chins and
noses
Streaks of green, streaks of light
Potters Bar now in sight
Eyes swivel
PRESS to OPEN
A shift all round
And out they tumble,
Stumble, rumble, mumble.

SOME AIR

Trees and sky

Slipping by
Hedges, fields
Parks and benches
Gardens greet
Precise and neat

Soon, soon beloved fields
Our church our school
The Entech pines
Yes, all the signs!

Returning to our village fond
Spacious green and quiet pond
And here my street

AND AIR

And air so sweet.

Edward and Sarah Deards shelling peas in the back garden of 15 Bridge Road soon after the war.

Wickfield Close

Turning left into Longmead, we find the Woolmer Green Sheltered Housing Scheme of Wickfield Close. Some 44 properties come under the scheme, the aim of which is to allow residents to live independently whilst receiving the support of a warden. When the warden is off duty the Communications Centre at Welwyn Garden City respond to the emergency calls from residents 24 hours a day, seven days a week throughout the year. The scheme is for residents but certain functions are open for non-sheltered housing scheme tenants. There is also an Over 55s Club which meets on Friday afternoons.

Mrs Flora Murray, first warden at the Wickfield Close bungalows, with her mother Mrs Hilda Ayres. Flora now does the teas for Busy Bees at the Village Hall each week on Wednesday.

The area at the front of Wickfield Close Community Centre showing the side of the Environmental Technology building.

The opening of Wickfield Close sheltered accommodation bungalows, taken in No. 5, home of Mrs Hilda Ayres. Left to right: Lady Brocket (who performed the opening ceremony), ?, Mrs Hilda Ayres, the architect, Paul Sapsed, Cllr Richard Smith.

The Pre-fabs

The pre-fabs were built after the VE Day celebrations on the waste ground off Bridge Road where Longmead and Wickfield Close now stand. Memories of living in the new houses remain vivid for many of Woolmer Green's residents. The following is just a small selection:

'We had a bonfire on the waste ground, Bridge Road, to celebrate end of war. Percy Jeffrey brought a whole lot of old tyres to burn. And did they burn! I don't think the fire stopped for a week!'

'I remember looking out of my mother's window and seeing them [the pre-fabs] being built.'

'The men built a small railway track round the area and sent the sections round on this… four sections and the walls were up… put a roof on and you had a house. It was fascinating to watch them constructed, about two or three a day would go up.'

'I was born in the pre-fabs, when the village was much smaller and a real community.'

'The pre-fabs were terribly cold in the winter but were very modern, with a fridge, a copper and a heated bathroom rail.'

'Pre-fabs had a good community spirit, everyone knew everyone else and the children used to play out on the green.'

'Pre-fabs were put up in 1947. It was very cold and coal was still rationed at the time. They were heated by pipes in the roof but this heating system really didn't work and the pre-fabs were notoriously cold.'

'The bathroom was the warmest place in the house as it had the heated towel rail.'

'It was very cold that winter and I went to Welwyn, Mill Lane and got a little stove, spending the divi on it and got the paraffin over at the garage at two shillings a week.'

'We moved into pre-fabs in January 1947. The houses were in a semi circle with a green in the middle. There were 36 houses all together. Some people had moved in before Christmas but there was no electricity.'

'I was on the Council list and moved from Digswell, it was Welwyn Rural District Council then.'

'We had utility furniture which was good and solid but plain: we couldn't get carpets as everything was in short supply. There was lino for the two bedrooms and bathroom and a bit of bomb damaged lino for the living room.'

'The kitchen was very modern, with kitchen units, a sink and a fridge under the draining board, a copper which was disguised by a fitted lid and two doors to get to the controls and an electric cooker. It was luxury but so very cold, perhaps because it was aluminium. There was no heat in the airing cupboard, the heat didn't circulate from the coal fire.'

'We were really pleased though to get the pre-fab and I was the envy of everybody as there was a beautiful bathroom, two bedrooms, lots of cupboard space, a large living room and a big garden. It was mostly young couples who got the houses. So they all started out together bringing up families. They were pulled down in 1967.'

'My brother lived there in the pre-fabs, didn't look nice from outside but were nice inside, little palaces. No central heating, no hot water.'

'At the coronation street party the children had sandwiches, jelly and ice cream and a big plate of lovely cream cakes.'

'The Council office was in Old Welwyn and the rent man used to come round every Tuesday.'

'The children went to Cubs and Boy Scouts. All the boys used to go off to play in the woods. Mums would keep an eye out for all the children not just their own. Children weren't locked out during the day and there were more mums about.'

'Wickfield Close pre-fabs had a street party on the green in the middle.'

'Mrs Orton's father Mr Archer was the coalman. His coalyard was where the path leads from Bridge Road to garages.'

'We used woods as a playground. The playing field was my grandfather's land. He planted the field up by hand. It was given or rented to the village.'

'Mr Wallace gave the land for the Recreation Ground to the village.'

'Grandfather farmed land near the playing field, he could walk on his land from The Ironhouse to Digswell.'

Longmead was erected in the 1960s by the Rural District Council and featured in their publicity (*below*) as an example of good modern housing. Prior to this there had been Moss' scrapyard on the site.

 The children who lived in the pre-fabs in 1953.

Carol Cooke and Margaret Bowes in Wickfield Close, c.1953. At the time of writing, Margaret is the caretaker of St Michael's School.

Carol Cooke in 1952, dressed for her first communion, aged seven. The picture was taken in a pre-fab. Note the old television set in the background – it was very important to be photographed in front of that!

Coronation party, 1953, on the green in front of the pre-fabs. Included in the photograph are: Joan Slater, Violet Deards, Doris Aldridge, Tuse Bennett, Mrs Hoar, Mrs Fletcher, Mrs Mardell, Nina Hoar, Ruth Spencer, Phillip Fletcher and Joan Bennett.

The boys are obviously enjoying their sandwiches!

This pre-fabs coronation photograph shows Nellie Smith, Mrs Mardell, Bill Cooke, Mrs Beck, Bridget Cooke, Mrs Shadbolt, Dan Cooke, Carol Cooke, Malcolm Shadbolt and Alan Jordan.

192

19 50

Hertford.

13th February, *19* 50

The Welwyn Parish Council.

To

Longmores.

As to Purchase of Recreation Ground at Woolmer Green from
Messrs. W. and R. Wallace for the sum of £435.

For professional services between

30th March *19* 48 and 20th Dec., *19* 49
in investigating title and preparing
and completing Conveyance..........

£ 10.13. 0.

The following payments have also

been made on Client's behalf:-

Search Fees............... -. 6. 0.
Postages and Incidentals.. -.10. 0.

-.16. 0.

£ 11. 9. 0.

Council Offices,
Welwyn-By-Pass Road,
Welwyn, Herts.

*Woolmer Green Playing Field
Capital A/c.*

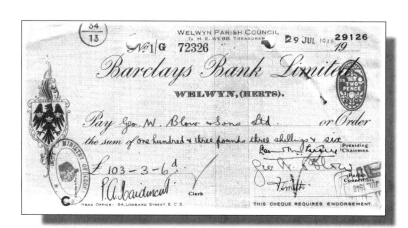

✳ *The land for the recreation
ground was sold to Welwyn
Parish Council in 1950 for £435 by
W. & R. Wallace. However, the
land must have been loaned or
rented to the Parish Council before
this since the Council paid for a
slide to be erected in February
1948 at the cost of £135.*

✳ *A cheque made out to Geo.
W. Blow & Sons to cover
various repairs and alterations to
the playground, 1948.*

Bridge Road to the Village Hall

At the end of Bridge Road and also in London Road were a number of thatched cottages which have long since disappeared. Here Widow Haggar and Mary Sadler plaited straw for hats as cottage outworkers. Fireplaces had a metal hook fixed at the side where straw was attached and plaited; the plaits were then taken by foot or horse and cart to Luton where they were used in the straw-hat industry. Strawplaiters Close is named in their memory.

On the right is the entrance to the new Village Hall and Recreation Ground. There had been a recreation ground and wooden pavilion here for some time and the entrance to the playing field was down a passage next to Tyler's fencing factory.

Local children played in the big park in Bridge Road where there was the large field and a hard-standing area with a slide, a roundabout and six swings. The children would go out on their bikes to the 'big rec' where there was a climbing frame, roundabout and a 'sky-high' slide. When they were a bit older they would play over on the heath and in the woods. Some residents remember the time when there were no such luxuries: 'There were no swings in the village if we wanted to play on the swings we had to walk over to Datchworth.'

The old pavilion burnt down during the 1980s and, after the old Village Hall was declared unsafe, there was great controversy over the building of a new hall by Welwyn Parish Council, not least over its siting. An access road was constructed along the site of the footpath to the recreation ground.

When the new facility finally opened in 1990, the event was covered in the *Welwyn and Hatfield Times*:

TV BARRY GIVES VILLAGE HALL RAVE REVUE

Television film critic Barry Norman gave a glowing review to the new £600,000 Woolmer Green village hall as he officially opened it on Saturday. More than 200 people, including head dignitaries, attended the ceremony at the hall, standing in Hall Lane, off Bridge Road, Woolmer Green. And they heard Barry, of Bury Lane, Datchworth, praise the development as a 'very impressive' structure.

Barry Norman, who unveiled a commemorative plaque, is pictured at the village hall entrance being greeted by Mrs Magdalene Benson, the parish council chairman. She received a basket of flowers to mark her birthday. Other council members are pictured in the background.

Welwyn Hatfield Council Chairman Jack Lonergan and his wife and representatives of local associations and businesses attended.

The public can view the hall at a Village Day on Saturday, December 1, between 2.30 pm and 4.30 pm, followed by a bonfire and firework display at 5 pm

and an evening barbeque organised by Woolmer Green Youth Club.

Another report from the same paper, 5 December 1990, reads:

HALL TOGETHER NOW

Woolmer Green village hall opened up its doors for the first time at the weekend. Hundreds of local residents flocked through the doors of the brand new building to sneak a preview at what some of the clubs and societies will be up to over the next year. Local Brownies, the aerobics club and the badminton club, to name but a few were on hand to recruit members.

"It's a lovely building," said George Clark, Clerk to Welwyn Parish Council, "Everyone seemed very pleased with it."

Work on the hall was started ten months ago when the old one – due to be demolished in January – became run down and unsafe to use any longer.

The new hall never became the centre for village activities to the same extent that the old one had been, but it is much admired by the public. When Woolmer Green Parish Council was formed in 2000 the new body took over the running and the maintenance of the hall. There have been extensive repairs to carry out although the hall has generally worn very well. A good range of activities take place, but there is still room for more, particularly from the village.

At the time of writing, the following activities are enjoyed in the hall: Brownies, sequence dancing, carpet bowls, badminton, Parish Council meetings, a clinic, toddler group (Busy Bees), Gardening Club, Women's Institute, t'ai chi instruction, dancing class and yoga.

Barry Norman performs the opening ceremony at the new Village Hall and shakes hands with Cllr Magdalene Benson, Chairman of Welwyn Parish Council. Joyce Catlin, Doug Dietrich, Madge Norman and David Parker can also be seen.

BROWNIES

 Brownie pack holiday in 1991.

 Brownie revels, 1991.

Brownie revels at Knebworth Park in 1990.

Brownie fun day at Datchworth, 1999.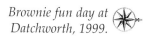

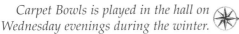

SEQUENCE DANCING, GARDENING & CARPET BOWLS

✴ *Jack and Peter Webber showed their models at the Craft Show.*

Carpet Bowls is played in the hall on Wednesday evenings during the winter. ✴

✴ *Marie Day wins the garden show cup in 1992. Shirley Staniforth is the chairman of the club which meets once a month and has a variety of speakers and interesting demonstrations. A garden show is normally held once a year; in 2001 the show was open to all villagers for the first time.*

Molly and Arthur Cummings sequence dancing in the hall at the Millennium Dance.

Sequence Dance Club masked ball, November 1999.

Present-day members of the WI. Left to right, standing: P. Smalley, D. Watts, J. Webber, C. Loader, E. Moody, J. Currell, M. Gregory, J. Dietrich, M. Norman, R. Hipgrave; seated: H. Holdsworthy, E. Orton, J. Catlin, D. Tyler, G. Firth, D. Croft, B. Giddens, S. Tjong, E. Randles, S. Staniforth.

The WI put on this fancy-dress party in the hall in about 1938. Peggy Brown's mother, Mrs Sarling, is the blacked-out lady holding the doll, 2nd from the left, 3rd row from the top; on the 2nd row from the top 4th along is Mrs Pettit and on the front row with the dark glasses is Mrs Monroe. It looks like Mrs Beard in the middle of the front row. It is quite interesting trying to decide what they were dressed as!

Woolmer Green
Craft Fair
9th November 1996

Do you have a Hobby that
you would like to Exhibit?

If so, we would like to hear from you!
Free to Exhibitors
(if you are selling we ask for a small
contribution)

Contact Judith
Winfield on
813897 for
further details

CRAFT SHOWS & CONCERTS AT THE VILLAGE HALL

Following the tradition set by artists and craftsmen who have lived in Woolmer Green in the past, including Harry Macdonald and Mrs Swincow, the village is still host to a number of artists and craftspeople. Exhibitors at one of the many Craft Shows organised by the Residents Association were:

The Webber family (wonderful models)
The Brownies
Denis Currell (more wonderful models)
The WI (with all their amazing skills on display including demonstrations of lace making and paper work)
Ian Chipperfield (superb photography around Woolmer Green)
David and Judith Watson (a mixed bag)
Linda Jacquet (decorated glass)
Betsy Linnett (another mixed bag for sale)
The Nursery Group
Enid Fairhead and David Thom (paintings)
Delia Scott (dried flowers)

Musical concerts have also been a great success and now that we have a piano for the hall we hope to continue them in years to come.

Enid Fairhead, a talented local painter, whose work has been hung in the Royal Academy.

Carys Wundowa and Katie Allard at the Craft Show in 1993.

Model aeroplanes made from cornflake packets by Eddy Vinall are admired by Ian May and Sam Breakwell.

Richard Jacquet, a talented musician, composer and organist of repute, and David Watson played piano duets at one of the Music Concerts.

63

WOOLMER GREEN & OAKLANDS YOUTH CLUB

Joker packs 'em in!

TV joker Jeremy Beadle was in the frame when it came to opening a village youth club's new building.

The star of Beadle's About and You've Been Framed performed a ribbon-cutting ceremony on Saturday at Woolmer Green and Oaklands Youth Club in Hall Lane.

Helping him carry out the task was brownie Rebecca Moone, eight, of London Road, Woolmer Green.

Jeremy proved a big hit, staying for almost three hours

meeting the crowd, including nine-week-old Joely Maguire (pictured). He also helped draw a raffle.

Club secretary Lindsey Moffatt said: "Most of the children were quite star struck and he was wonderful with them.

"He's got a way with people and children in particular. He was extremely jovial and well accepted by the crowd."

The 11 to 19-year-old youngsters, who have been without a base for over a year, will meet in the building every Thursday.

Jeremy Beadle opens the Youth Club in 1995.
The Youth Club had met for a long time in the old Village Hall under the eye of Harold Edwards (who ran the club for two nights each week). Members recall roller-skating in the old hall. Sadly, the group found things very difficult when the new hall was built and eventually it was forced to close. Due to the efforts of Alison and Steve Henderson, an old terrapin building was located in Hatfield and local people loaded it onto a truck and transported it to Woolmer Green where it was re-erected at the back of the hall. Long discussions took place over where it should be erected and extensive reinforced concrete foundations were built for the hut so that it wouldn't fall over when the trains went past! It was eventually opened by Jeremy Beagle. The club is classed as a charity under the auspices of Herts County Council Youth Service; a Management Committee from the village and a Youth Management Committee oversee the club's activities and look after the building.

Local Government & the Creation of Woolmer Green Parish

Parish Councils were formed in 1894; prior to that all parish affairs were looked after by the church but the split allowed civil matters to be looked after by a specially-elected council, quite separate from the Parochial Church Council. Over 100 years later these two bodies are still being confused.

The Rural District Councils were formed to take care of matters outside the scope of Parish Councils and Welwyn Rural District Council had its offices on the land between Godfrey Davis and the A1M (not yet built). There were 14 members on the Rural District Council drawn from Welwyn, Digswell, Mardley Heath and Woolmer Green. In addition there were 13 councillors on Welwyn Parish Council and yet only one from the area on Hertfordshire County Council.

Mrs Archer

Mrs Archer *(right)* and Mr P. Long *(see page 125)*, were both representatives on the Rural District Council. Peter Long remembers Mrs Archer giving his father a lift to District Council meetings and being told off for this since they belonged to different political parties. He also tells of the crowds which gathered round his father's gate when the District Council put the rates up by 1d.

Edward Ellison Bigge, who lived at Gun Lodge (where Monread Nursing Home now stands), William Beechener and John King *(see page 129)* were among the first parish councillors for Woolmer Green on Welwyn Parish Council. Later on Mrs E.J. Beard of 15 Garden Road (who wrote an excellent book on Woolmer Green) and Mr A.G. Swinscow of Paynes Farm were councillors and they were instrumental in getting the land around the pond declared Common Land.

Before the formation of our own parish we had two councillors representing Woolmer Green Ward on Welwyn Parish Council. This had been reduced from three some time during the 1900s. Quite often, sadly, Woolmer Green did not have a representative of its own on Welwyn Parish Council.

During the 1990s Singh Grewal, Michael Loader, Steve Henderson, Andy Moffat and Judith Watson represented Woolmer Green Ward. The formation of our new parish took some years during which the Residents' Association were very active in the village. This had been formed at the end of the 1980s by Enid Fairhead, first Chairman, and Doug Dietrich to try to focus local opinion regarding the replacement of the old hall by a new building specific to villagers' needs. They had little success with this but the Association then set up clubs in the newly-opened hall, supported the Youth Club, planted trees and flowers, liaised with outside bodies such as the Police, raised money for the restoration of the pond, and more. Mr Hipgrave still looks after the village planters.

There were various speakers at the Annual Meetings regarding becoming our own parish and, following on from this, the Committee decided to canvass the village. Certainly the desire for a separate parish wasn't unanimous; however, a first attempt was made during the creation of the Unitary Authorities only for the Government to pull out of its commitment.

The Residents' Association Committee included Enid Fairhead, Sheila Rogers, Peter Fletcher, Christine Blackman, Kathy Stevens, Judith Watson, Linda Jacquet and Frances Trevor who all spent many long hours working out all the ramifications of independence.

April 2000 saw the transfer of the Woolmer Green share of funds from Welwyn Parish Council and in May six councillors were elected to Woolmer Green Parish to look after all affairs until the next election. Council meetings are held bi-monthly in the hall and are open to the public. The Parish Council has an advisory role on Planning Applications and has responsibility for the Village Hall, the two play areas and the Jolly Garden.

✳ *Members of the Residents' Association, Joan Dietrich, Graham Wilshere and Enid Fairhead, working on the Jolly Garden.*

Woolmer Green's first Parish Council. Left to right: Terry Singer, Enid Fairhead, Tina Jolly (Hon. Minutes Secretary), Alan Manley, Judith Watson, Rosemary Cooper (Clerk), Sheila Rogers, Jane Thom.

ROW OVER VILLAGE SPLIT BID

VILLAGERS wanting to break away from their parish council say they can turn round the fortunes of their local hall.

Woolmer Green's residents' association has been canvassing opinions on leaving Welwyn Parish Council and setting up its own authority.

It believes the move would cut staffing costs at the recently-built £600,000 village hall, which will lose £24,000 this year.

If successful, the group hopes to apply for grants to create a stage and even an IT centre in the hall.

Residents would also save on the overheads of a larger council and the grounds maintenance of public land in Welwyn, the association claims.

Spokeswoman Sheila Rogers, of

By DERYN SUMMERS

New Road, Woolmer Green, said: "I have only had one person not in favour and everyone else going round canvassing is finding exactly the same thing.

"We are quietly confident that we can use the hall much more economically, without the large overheads that we have to pay because of the staffing on Welwyn Parish Council.

"People wouldn't be going out to the village with this petition if they weren't confident it would be better value for money."

But district and county councillor Richard Smith warned the move could see a substantial rise in council tax on Woolmer Green's 490 houses.

A band D property currently pays £27 towards services, making up

£20,000 of Welwyn parish's £120,000 budget.

But bills might need to double to cover the hall's losses and provide a small budget, he believes.

He said: "I want the people of Woolmer Green to be fully informed of the consequences of a break away.

"I understand that a community, which Woolmer Green certainly is, might want to have its own local council.

"I think Welwyn parish as well administered, does a good job and I would be sorry to see it break up into small parts."

The association needs to collect 250 signatures which will then be sent to Welwyn Hatfield Council for consideration. The district council is likely to hold its own consultation exercise before reaching a decision."

The beginning of independence for Woolmer Green,
1997. The following year, in October, this report was printed in the Welwyn and Hatfield Times:

A village is a step closer to having its own parish council after a recent decision by Welwyn Hatfield Councillors. Results of a questionnaire to residents of Woolmer Green showed those against the move were outnumbered by two to one. Councillors agreed at a recent policy and resources committee meeting for a working party to put together draft regulations for the proposed new parish. These cover such things as its boundary, the number of councillors, electoral arrangements and the impact on Welwyn Parish. Woolmer Green Parish Council has its office at the hall. There are six councillors who are elected every four years, the next election being in 2003.

It wasn't always easy to convince people that we could run our own affairs.

Do you want independence?

VILLAGERS are being asked for their views on breaking away from their current parish council.

Woolmer Green's residents' association has been collecting the views of its 950 voters on whether to form its own parish or stay part of Welwyn.

The village, which has 500 homes, has grown in the last few years and the move would give it its own identity, "Yes" campaigners believe.

The Beautiful Game: Woolmer Green Rangers Football Club

The first mention of a football club in Woolmer Green was in September 1901; the President was Mr Bigge of Gun Lodge. The first picture we have is from 1923 (*overleaf*) with Woolmer Green Football Club wearing their distinctive V-neck strip. Nob Tyler remembers some of their names: Stan Males, ? Moss, Charlie Young (Capt.), Wally Nutting, ?, Charlie Skeggs, ? Kingham, Horace Nutting, Albert Draper and Freddy Sharp. Before there was a football field at the Recreation Ground the teams played on the land behind Mardleybury Pond and also on the land at the end of Robbery Bottom Lane, where the gasometers used to stand and where the footpath to Datchworth starts; their changing room was an old metal caravan. The team moved to the Recreation Ground when the farm was demolished and the land was bought from Mr Wallace.

The club was re-formed in early April 1974 in the Saloon Bar of the Chequers with the first officers being Len English (Chairman), David Brownsell (Hon. Secretary), Ron Britten (Hon. Treasurer) and Terry Hollands (Manager). The club was accepted into the North Herts Football Association and put into Division Five. They played and won their first game in September 1974 3-0 against Paynes Park FC, from Hitchin. In the 1975–76 season, the club won the Division Five trophy and were then promoted to Division Three after being runners up in Division Four. More trophies came their way in 1977–78, with the club winning the Division Three title and the next year the Division Two championship. After a brief hiatus, the club won the First Division championship in 1986–87, then the North Herts Benevolent League Shield for the first time in 1991–92. Having waited 20 years to do so they then held on to the title for the ensuing two years. They won the shield again in 1996–97 and in 1999–2000, as well as the North Herts League Greg Cup in 1993–94 and in 1996–97.

During the successful late 1970s it was decided to start up a reserve team which was run by Dave Hartley and Terry Sage and won the Reserve Cup three times – in the 1990–91, 1992–93 and 1995–96 seasons.

On the death of Len English, Dave Hartley became the new Chairman. Terry Sage was made the new Treasurer on the retirement of Ron Britten. Peter Gillard from Knebworth then took on the job of Secretary for three seasons, doing a wonderful job. Sadly, during the mid 1990s, Mr Hartley died. It was decided to reorganise the club and Mr Brownsell took over the Secretary's job with Jason Cloatt being the new Manager. Mr Brownsell would like a special mention made of two great stalwarts of the club, Martin Helman and his son Lawrence who managed both teams during the late 1980s.

This photograph show the old pavilion, the base of which still stands at the entrance to the Recreation Ground. It burnt down in the 1980s. Here the Captain is receiving the cup at the old pavilion in 1963. Johnny Buckle and David Brownsell are included.

Why Charles is Looking for Another Line-Up (Welwyn Hatfield Times, 1970s)

These likely lads are all in their 70s and 80s now – and former centre half Charles Skeggs would like to hear from them.

Mr Skeggs is pictured in the centre of the middle row of the Woolmer Green football team of 1923.

At his home in Kingsdale House, Welwyn, he told me: "We didn't win any prizes but we had a lot of fun.

"I'd like to arrange a reunion, if any of the players live in the Welwyn area."

Though he gave up playing in the 1930s, 82-year-old Mr Skeggs still enjoys watching football on the television.

Watching the England team of today probably brings back memories of the village football team of half a century ago.

Woolmer Green Rangers line up to celebrate their triumph, 1963.

Woolmer Green Rangers Captain receiving the cup in 1964 at the old pavilion on the Recreation Ground.

Woolmer Green Rangers in 1964.

 In the 1964–65 season, Woolmer Green were very honoured to be visited by Cliff Jones and Dave Mackay from Tottenham Hotspur. Woolmer Green Rangers Charity Cup final at Woolmer Green Playing Field 1964–65. Left to right, back: Cliff Jones, Joey Creighton, Mick Brownsell, Nobby Burlingham, Gaffer Gayle, Brian Manning, Richard Lawrence, Dave Mackay; front: ?, Brian Carrick, Bill Giddens, Vic Meech, Alan Ephgrave.

Woolmer Green Rangers in 1989.

Woolmer Green players, 1970–71, winners of Welwyn Hatfield Sunday League Cup, finalists of Welwyn Hospital Cup 1973–74 and 1974–75. Left to right, back row: Johnny Buckle, Bill Giddens, Ges Rulton, Malachy de Lacy, Graham Hewitt, Danny Milliken, Alby Thomason, David Herd, Frank Coan, Harold Edwards; front: Alan Ephgrave, Steve Kibler, Brian Carrick (Captain), Gary Giddens (mascot), Leon Poulton, Vic Meech, Hugh de Lacy.

Woolmer Green Rangers with the shield in 1992. Left to right, back row: ?, Mark Company, Ken Evans, Andy Saker, ?, Danny Kennoy, Chris Farley, Sean Gillard, ?, Tony Hatfield, Greg Evans, Terry Sage, Dave Brownsell; front: Andrew Klimek, Andy Sandford, Trevor Campion, Mouse, Steve Deards.

Woolmer Green Youth Football team in 1993, sponsored by Lisles Garage. Left to right, back: Jodie Jennings, David Chapman, Ian May, Sam Breakwell, Peter North, Ben Lake; front: Steven Aldridge, Danny Kennoy, Michael Langsley, Stuart Hobbs, Joe de Lacy, Ben Cunningham.

Woolmer Green with the Benevolent Shield won for the third year in succession in 1994. Left to right, back: Mark Klimek, Dave Matson, Greg Evans, Martin Mitchell, Chris Farley, Tony Cotterall, Pat Chester, Andrew Klimek; front: Simon Bain, Paul Walsh, Mark Smith, Ian Bloomquist, Gary Plummer.

Woolmer Green Reserves in 1994.

Woolmer Green Rangers, 2000–2001. Sadly, Woolmer Green Rangers isn't really a village team anymore.
Two other teams also use the village as their home ground: White Hart and Sellers.

PART THREE

Approaching Woolmer Green from the North

The Great North Road looking north through the village in 1951. This part of the road has seen a lot of change in the last 100 years, mainly due to Woolmer Green's position on the A1. There were numerous garages and workshops for motorcycles, cars and lorries, and cafes and stop-overs for drivers were also built. The cars have been identified as follows: 1938 Ford Anglia (far left of picture), 1930/31 Austin 7 Ruby Saloon (behind the Anglia), 1931/32 Riley 9 Monaco (filling up), 1947/48 Vauxhall 14HP (parked far right).

Monread Lodge
Residential and
Nursing Home.

The Great North Road

Woolmer Green starts immediately you leave Knebworth on the London Road. Indeed, the last couple of houses on the left-hand side of the road are actually in Woolmer Green.

On the right is Monread Lodge Residential and Nursing Home, purpose-built in the late 1990s on the site of the Great North Road Hotel and with rooms for 60 people in need of care.

The Great North Road Hotel as pictured in the shilling guidebook published by Welwyn Rural District Council entitled Rural England. The advertisement carried the hotel's phone number – Knebworth 3167 – and listed the 'proprietress' as E.M. Dow.

The riding school attached to the hotel continued for some years after the hotel was destroyed by fire.

KNEBWORTH STABLES
Knebworth • Herts

Miss E. D. SHELDON
Knebworth 2201
(Adjoining above Hotel)

TUITION IN ALL BRANCHES OF EQUITATION • HUNTER HACKS & PONIES ALWAYS FOR HIRE OR SALE HORSES TAKEN AT LIVERY • HUNTS ATTENDED & GYMKHANAS DURING THE SEASON

Over 200 Rosettes Won during 1948 and 1949

*The Great North Road Hotel in the 1930s and (inset) china bought when
North Lodge was sold up in 1913/14.*

*Jean Knowles, now Jean Webber, is taking the picture of her sister's wedding at the Great North Road Hotel in 1963.
Monread Lodge Nursing Home stands here now. This site has been much sought after by developers since The Great
North Road Hotel burnt down soon after this picture was taken. Prior to being run as an hotel, the buildings were in
private use; Mr and Mrs Bigge lived there around 1900 and did a great deal for the village, paying for children to go
off on outings and to garden parties at Danesbury. The residents prior to the Bigges are thought to have been Mr and
Mrs Cotton who then moved to Payne's Farm.*

The 1930s house in front of Entech.

LIGHT INDUSTRY

Environmental Technology now occupies the first factory on the right as Woolmer Green is approached from Knebworth. The first building began in 1908 as a condensed, or evaporated, milk factory known as the White Cross Dairy, opened by the Countess of Lytton, being then part of the Knebworth Estate. Milk was collected from farms within a six-mile radius, separated, sterilised and reduced in bulk. It was then sent to London where sterilised water was added before delivery.

It was claimed that the processed milk would keep from 12 to 36 hours longer than ordinary milk. Production continued until about 1936. One local recalls that in the 1920s the Dutch Manager, Mr Blogg, lived in the Manager's house at the front of the factory and that 'the dense pine wood was supposed to scent the milk.' Sadly, the majority of pines blew down in the hurricane of 1987. Another resident remembers a variety of products being made on the site, including 'artificial fertiliser and then gun-powder and munitions... during the war.'

Later the factory became a testing laboratory for interface material used in the tailoring industry and fabrics were received from many of the up-market London stores such as Harrods to be tested for both strength and fire resistance.

Subsequently, in a similar vein, it was known as Trubro House where stiff collars for shirts were made. The material came from Donegal to a factory in Hemel Hempstead and thence to Woolmer Green. At this time there were 'big metal presses for cutting out all the materials, three layers of it to make the stiff collars.' Some of the work was done by outworkers in the village.

Environmental Technology took over in 1981. They are an architectural design firm who are involved in many of the amazing modern buildings such as Canary Wharf and the Jubilee Line stations.

The first factory on the left which is now occupied by Lessiters was originally used by a firm called Vendustrial which made coffee machines and catering equipment; it was a big employer in the village. Later it was taken over by a firm which manufactured valves. They had a big advert on the wall for 'Naff' valves, so it wasn't really surprising that they closed!

The building was then taken over by Lessiters, manufacturers of speciality chocolate. Liquid chocolate is imported in bulk from Switzerland and the mouth-watering chocolates are made on the premises.

Pines in front of Entech House before and after the storm of 1994.

*Two views of the same stretch of road with about 40 years separating them. The top picture shows an agricultural village with an unmetalled road surface; only banks define the edge of the road. The lower picture (c.1951) shows the same barn at the end of Bridge Road but Lisles Garage is now dominant. The house on the left of the garage was knocked down during the garage expansion in the 1990s to make room for a larger display of cars. Note the road markings: three lanes throughout – left side, right side and 'suicide' in the middle.
The footpaths look in a much better state of repair than they are now.*

People from Woolmer Green at the Sainsbury's depot at Creasey's Garage in 1942, together with the lorry drivers. Included are: Mr Holmes, Joan Bennett, Queenie Oak, Peggy Larman, Mrs Kaye, Mr Nash, Freddie Oakman and Daphne Stammers.

This Shell station was opposite Lisles, where Wickfield is today. Coalman Herbie Groom had the bungalow just before the garage; his coal yard was next to Lisles Passage.

This wooden house used to stand where Barleycroft is today, once the home of Agatha Ansell. Mr and Mrs Hands also lived in the cottage and used to do the cooking for the Jubilee Cafe. During the war snacks were sold to lorry drivers from a wooden shack nearby.

One of Creasey's lorries used for transporting forage for John Inns who owned the Twin Foxes site at one time. This photograph was taken outside their garage in Knebworth between the Chinese Takeaway and the Co-op. Creasey's had a number of outlets in the area and one resident recalls the sign above their garage 'Humber, Hillman, Sunbeam-Talbot'.

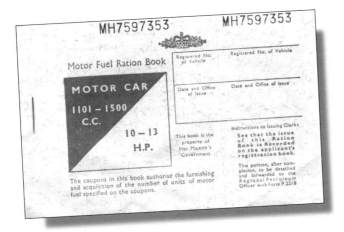

LISLES GARAGE

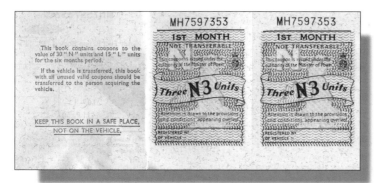

Wartime rationing on petrol meant that motor use was restricted to necessary journeys only.

The first photograph of Lisles Garage taken in the 1920s. The company was established as long ago as 1900 by William Lisles as an engineering works and motor-repair shop. The original twin-roofed workshops still exist today as the showrooms. In 1917 S.F. Deards joined Lisles as an apprentice. 'The pump attendant would ask you if you wanted air or oil,' one old customer recalled, 'which would be done for 6d.' In 1939, Mr Deards took over control of the company and it has remained in his family ever since. The Monte Carlo Rally used to pass the doors of Lisles and Ray Cox, then a young boy, would help by filling the oil bottles for the passing competitors.

Every gentleman's pride and joy: 'Wash your windscreen, sir?' In the 1950s Lisles became one of the first petrol stations in the country to have a canopy. On the left is a 1948/50 Ford Pilot and on the right is a Jaguar 1.5 litre. One day a lorry came along and knocked the little wooden cabin off its concrete base, so the owners drove another lorry to the other side and pushed it back on again!

The side of the workshops in July 1951.

 The cars in the showroom are Morris or Wolseley 12/14 HP from 1947.

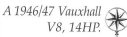

A 1946/47 Vauxhall V8, 14HP.

Spare engines and every part you could want were all kept to hand.

Another shot of the side of the workshops. The car panels were all hand-beaten in those days. At the back of the picture is a Bedford QL 4X4 Recovery; the middle row of cars includes: a Bedford 'U' type drop-side (1948/50), a Ford Prefect (1953/54), a Ford Zephyr 6, an Austin pick-up (1948/52), a Ford V8 Pilot (1947/50), a Morris 12HP.

 Digging the hole for the new petrol tanks when Lisles was renovated in the early 1990s.

This Esso hoarding across the road from Lisles is where Wickfield (top) now stands. At one time, with Wickfield Filling Station which stood here, Lisles had stations on either side of the road!

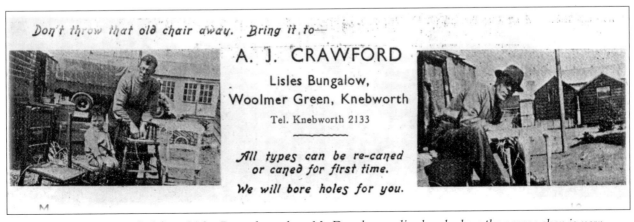

Don't throw that old chair away. Bring it to —

A. J. CRAWFORD

Lisles Bungalow,
Woolmer Green, Knebworth

Tel. Knebworth 2133

All types can be re-caned
or caned for first time.

We will bore holes for you.

The chair caner worked from Lisles Bungalow where Mr Deards once lived and where the garage shop is now.

37 London Road

I wrote to 37 london road. I had a Reply From Mr and Mrs chamber 37 london road has 4 windows and a door at Front. The house is called White Gabers it was built in 1897. On 37 london Road chimney which have Strechers.

They say there house used to be three very small cottages.

Mrs Archer with son, Terry, outside their house which is now No.41, c.1934. Compare this with the photograph on the opposite page which clearly shows the structure of the three original houses. No.39 was where Eileen Archer (now Orton) was born. It was then a wooden cottage. After this was knocked down the 'top shop' was built; it was still operating very successfully in the early 1990s when it closed.

Life on the London Road

The houses on the east side of London Road were originally cottages and each of the present-day houses held three families. Memories of growing up here abound. One resident recalled that:

A footpath led by Lisles Garage to Paynes Farm which was just wide enough for a pushchair. Along each side of the path were the allotments which were beautifully tended. Many had a small shed for tools and a deckchair and quite a few plots included a tiny lawn and area for flowers. Sweet William was widely cultivated in the area.

The resident at No. 23 remembered that:

Quite a large bomb fell there in wartime, I understand root crops came through back windows of the London Road cottages. Mrs White was bombed on the main road behind the two houses near the bus stop. Incendiaries were dropped which lit up the sky like it was daytime.

Eileen Archer (now Orton) having a bath in 1928 in the wooden house where No.39 now stands.

Eileen Archer in her aeroplane outside her home in London Road.

 Fine Fare, better known as the 'top shop', 1956.

Looking across to the brick pillar box outside 1, Bridge Road, from the 'top shop'. Ian and Jean Chipperfield lived above the shop.

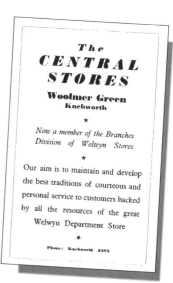

The CENTRAL STORES

Woolmer Green
Knebworth

★

Now a member of the Branches Division of Welwyn Stores

★

Our aim is to maintain and develop the best traditions of courteous and personal service to customers backed by all the resources of the great Welwyn Department Store

★

Phone: Knebworth 2383

There's a never ending procession of savings at Fine Fare.

FINE FARE
Where you can be fair to your family and your purse.

Inside the 'top shop' in 1956. The cat used to lie in the corner near where the bacon sides were hanging.

31 London Road.

I wrote to number 31 London Road. I got a reply from Mrs Ros Horsley. The house is yellow and has two windows at the top that are small. The window style is Georgian. At the side of the house there is a little room there is a window in the room. At the side of the house there is a door and a light at the side of the door high up. The lamp style is coach. A round the windows and the door is white.

Mrs Ros Horsley look at her record and it said in 1865 there were some wooden cottages. In 1910 the cottage. In 1910 the cottages were burned down. Two more cottages were built on that site. The cottages were built in brick. The two cottages were owned by John Wallis and sons. The two cottages were used for office and archives for the Redlands company.

Archives means someone how saves old folders with old history. And some-one how keeps old photos.

In 1976 to 79 the cottages were bought. The two cottages were bought by a welwyn couple. The two cottages were knocked into one house. No. 29 was no. 31 and it is 31

Then one of the couples parents, bought some cottages into one house and there house is now no. 37. Mrs Ros Horsley lived in 31 London Road for 5 years.

1 Bridge Road

The house I chose was occupied by Mrs Aitchinson.
The house is facing the A1. When Mr Jolly took the picture
the bank out side was being dug up because of the gas

The house is a fenish bond like this

The roof is a normal roof like this

The following information was received from the occupant of the house:

This house was built around 1700. Bridge Road didn't exist then, it was just a track towards Rabley Heath. The cottage's address then was Great North Road then London Road. Then in the 1940s the council sent me a letter stating my address was to be 1, Bridge Road. The cottage used to be 2 small cottages. In the 1800s a shoemaker called Fletcher came to live here and made it one dwelling and a workshop was at the back.
The main road was not so wide then. The green verge outside the cottage was quite extensive. At the beginning of the century there was a water pump on the corner by the front gate. There was also a water pump by the butcher's shop.
About 1938 a brick post box was erected at the corner. That was when the cottage was used as a Post Office for a few years, but the hours of opening were very limited.
Earlier there was a letterbox set into the wall of the village shop opposite.

My letter to number 23

I noticed that the house that I wrote to has shutters on either side of the window and a letter porch and that you have some thing in the garden which has a piece of wood holding a tier The tier has a man on it The wall was made of red bricks and the bricks are the same as the wall. they tier is still standing whar it was

17 LONDON ROAD

The house that I wrote to was 17 London Road unfortunately I did not receive a reply. It looks old at the front but at the side it looks newer than the front. On each side of the door they have got two lanterns. The band is a flemish bond. Their door has been to look likes its old but it is not old. The window ledges look worn out underneath. On the side of the house there is no bonding because it is pebble dashed.

Iain . J

Evergreen Lodge.

The house that I chose to write to is called Evergreen Lodge. I took a letter and I did not get a Reply because I did not go back and get the photos.

The house has two brown chimneys, white windows and a white door as well.

It stand's near a pond which has an is land in the middle and mature trees around the edge. In between the trees and the house there is a path and a small front garden which the dog can run up and down in.

THE FACTORY

Myomax were the first company to base their factory here. The brick frontage for production units was erected after the war. A fabric factory, Myomax came in handy because locals could 'get off-cuts there very cheaply and made lots of things from them.' By 1980 the factory was empty, the only people to go there being children who liked to play on the site. The final occupants had been a firm called Skiltons.

The Red Lion in the early 1900s. The earliest record of the pub dates back to 1780. It was bought by Henry Crabb of Hitchin, brewer, in 1818. It may have been rebuilt on what appears to have been its former ground plan about 1927 when the road was widened.

The Red Lion, early 1900s, showing the Fox twins on the right of the picture. The earlier building had a water trough and signpost in front. The twins are remembered in the naming of the Twin Foxes estate at the south of the village.

Ted and Walter Deards and friends outside the Red Lion in about 1900.

Ted and Walter Deards, hay tiers, outside the Red Lion c.1900 with the carts laden. Many of the old coaching inns provided changes of horses for travellers and the Chequers and the Red Lion probably did just this. To this end many of the fields surrounding the inns would have provided grazing land for their own and for customers' horses.

The Red Lion
26 London Road

The people who live there have been licensed tenants of the coope Benskins for about 8 years now. They took over Gavin Clarke who was working there for 5 years.

In the pub records it shows that in 1780 a Mr Robert Kent paid a poor rent of for the Red Lion. The Churrington diary refers to the pub at the beginning of the 19th century.

In 1836 the pub was rebuilt by a Pryor Reid who came from Hatfield.

Memories relating to the Red Lion include the following:
'My father worked behind the bar in the Red Lion, so tended to drink there: it was just local people.' (This recollection comes from Geoff Cox.)
'Darts and billiards were popular there.'
'Lorries used to park up at The Fox and round the Red Lion and what with all the garages Creasey's, Mosses Motor Mart, Wickfield Garage, etc. and cafés (Bobs Café) it was a busy place. The road and transport played a major part in the village.'

Woolmer Green.

Bishop, Photo.

The Great North Road looking north, early 1900s.

Dorothy Gregory in 1930 outside her house in London Road, now number 17, with Leslie and Derek. (See page 90.)

The listed milestone in the middle of the village.

WELWYN
PARISH
STEVENAGE 4
LONDON 27

Bishop, Photo.

At one time there were a number of general stores in the village all selling a great range of commodities. Among them was Grandpa Tucker's in Evergreen Close, which sold all sorts of oddments. One resident recalled: 'We bought some elaborate bootlaces from him, with which we tied up our hair.' A visiting fruitier came weekly from Knebworth, door to door.

The shop as it is today – a nail and beauty salon which is quite separate from the adjoining house.

OUTINGS

A village coach outing to Clacton in 1954.
Left to right, back: Nob and Vi Tyler, Jimmy and Rona Leggett, Mr and Mrs Leggett, Celia Higgins, Brian Stevens,
Cissy Davis, Daphne Harris, Mary Brinkley, Cissy English and Rennie, Peggy Harris, ?, George Brinkley, ?, ?,
Mrs Stevens, ?, Mrs English, ?, David Harris, Ms Harris, ?, Mrs Stevens' mother;
centre (bending forward): Joan Harris, Ann Leggett, Pat Edwards;
front: Barbara Stevens, Tony Barnard with Tish Tyler, John Harris, Bernie English, Mr Stevens, Mr Barrows,
Graham Stevens, Ronnie Davis, Gerald Harris, Albert English, Kathy English, Billy Tyler,
Hilda English, Mr English.

The yearly men's outing to the seaside in the 1920s. From the left: George Lisles, Dossy Mead, Phil Tyler,
Mr Burge, Mr Lisles, Mr Jackson, Mr Sharp, Johnny Burge, Charlie Nutting, Charlie Skeggs, Lefty Tyler, Nick
Ewington, Will Tyler, Charlie Groom, Ted Beechner (landlord of the Red Lion), Frank Slater, Mr Currell (driver).

In 1955 there was a re-run of the stagecoach from York to London through all the villages on the Great North Road. About nine coaches passed through the village each day on their way to the North.

Tap-dancing outing. Left to right, back: Mrs Smith, Mr and Mrs Beechner (landlord and landlady of Red Lion), Vera Gibbs, Mrs Tucker holding grandson Dennis, Mrs Monk, Mrs C. Tucker, Mrs D. Tucker with Jim (or Ron), Mrs Carter with Robin, Mrs Clements, Beryl Jackson, Cynthia Page, Mrs Archer, Mrs Regan, Mrs Snow, Fergus Brennon, Douglas Nutting, Raymond (pianist to the class);
centre: Joan Brownsell, Heather and Daphne Slith, Dorothy Page, Evelyn Tucker, Frederick Young, Frederick Day, Gladys Burge, ? Bonham, Dorothy Sharp, Hilda Clements, Rene Males, Eileen Archer, Jean Allot;
front: Jimmy Carter, Dorothy Tucker, Terry Archer, Petal Carter, Mary Snow, Allan Cracknel, Josephine Clements.

✴ The Groom family in 1927.
Len, Beatrice and Herbert Groom
and Mrs Tyler at the back; Granny
Groom and Chas Groom at the front
with Nob Tyler on his knee.

✴ Len and Herb Groom in the
1930s.

The Grooms

The Grooms came from Burnham
Green. Herbie had a coalyard
next to the garage and, together with
Mr Archer, used to supply the village; he lived in the bungalow to the
north of Lisles' garage. He used to
sing in the church choir when young
and started again when he was an
old man, singing regularly until just
before he died.

Tylers

Tylers, the butchers, had a very good reputation in Woolmer Green with people coming from as far away as Letchworth to place their orders. Mrs Tyler handled the financial side of the business and never handled meat. Mr Tyler is remembered as a big man and 'one of the best butchers in the area'. Locals remember 'fine fish and chips done by Mr Tyler' on a Tuesday behind the shop where Spencers had their mobile chippy.

✳ *Ernest Tyler, Nob Tyler's father, was brother to Will Tyler the butcher. He was a well-sinker and died down a well while still in his twenties. Albert Tyler went down the well to try and save his father but it was too late. On another occasion, a gypsy boy fell down a well at Welches Farm but also died. The boy is buried in the church-yard. Albert was given the George Medal by the King for his efforts.*

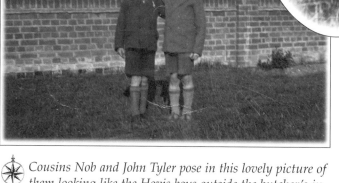

✳ *Cousins Nob and John Tyler pose in this lovely picture of them looking like the Hovis boys outside the butcher's in the 1920s; the wall is still there but it is now rendered. Today Nob and Vi's son, Roy Tyler, is one of the country's best clay-pigeon shooters and enters competitions all over the world.*

✳ *Will Tyler, the village butcher in the 1930s. Evidently he also took bets and Margaret Newton says that her mother, Lily, Will's daughter, used to get quite worried about this at times.*

✳ *The butcher's and the Fish Shop, now the architect's premises, together with Mr Tyler's house which was once a thatched cottage (see page 93).*

PART FOUR
Approaching Woolmer Green from the East

Bluebell time at Cave Wood as it was in 1990.

Mardleybury Manor & Farm

There are two ways into Woolmer Green from the east; one comes past Paynes Farm and down New Road, the other past Mardleybury, where the woods on the hill used to be even more delightful in the springtime. Mardleybury is one of the ancient manors mentioned in the Domesday Book and derives its name from an Anglo-Saxon word meaning 'the weasels' clearing'; it gave its name to a Norman owner, Alward de Mardeley.

The holding passed through several owners over the centuries until, in 1598, Sir William Lytton of Knebworth purchased certain lands belonging to 'Mardelye burye'; his family owning the adjacent manor of Knebworth since the time of Henry VIII. The manor of Mardleybury was thus a possession of the Lyttons for well over three centuries until Lady Hermione Cobbold, the elder daughter of the second earl and wife of Mr Cameron Cobbold, the Governor of the Bank of England, disposed of the property in 1950. It is a listed building.

Mardleybury Manor has been the scene of a number of 'reportings'. Recent occupants have had some odd experiences. While building a shed in the grounds two men lifted a heavy floor unit which they left propped up against the wall while they went away for a short break. When they came back the unit was in its original place although no one had been near it and it took two men to lift it.

Inside the house one room in particular seems to be haunted. The owner saw a scarf thrown on the bed which did not belong to her or any other person in the house. On another occasion an observer interested in ghosts and hauntings set out to listen for strange happenings. She said that she could hear ticking noises yet there were no clocks in the room. Cath Overman, who ran the nursery in the village for a long time, can tell of many things that happened to her.

One explanation for these happenings is that the house was built over a hidden spring which affects the foundations of the building.

Two centuries ago there was a grand party at the manor. One of the guests, a young lady, was being driven home in her carriage when the driver lost control of the horse and the carriage tipped over, spilling the young woman into the pond, where she drowned. So distinct is the ghost of the young woman at this spot that several motorists have reported braking hard to avoid her.

The farmhouse was built in 1914 by Lord Lytton and was designed by the school of Sir Edwin Lutyens (they were also the architects for the church). Lutyens had married one of Lord Lytton's sisters and as a result was always given any architectural work on the Knebworth Estate. The farmhouse was occupied by Walter Wallace who had many interests, including the extraction of gravel from Mardley Heath. He built up a pedigree herd of Hereford cattle which were housed in the marvellous barns still standing across the road and next to the mere or pond. The first barn, now housing the car-valeting business, is also listed.

Memories of Mardleybury include Mr Sapsed, the farmer, who 'did a lot for the village and let the schoolchildren sit in his cart and go and see the cows being milked.' During the war one would sometimes see planes hedge hopping, as pilots trained to fly low over the field along the road towards Datchworth – quite a frightening sight.

The road into Woolmer Green joins White Horse Lane and there are ghostly tales concerning this thoroughfare as well! Margaret Webber related:

One of my ancestors was on the wrong side during the Civil War and both he and his white charger were beheaded. Their heads were left to rot on poles. The white horse has often been seen and heard galloping down White Horse Lane.

There were gasometers, or gas-holders, at the junction of the footpath to Datchworth with White Horse Lane. The sewage works were also out here and this was where the last flying bomb of the war fell.

Looking across Mardleybury pond to the large barn.

Mardleybury Manor and the pond in the early 1900s. Mardleybury Pond has reserved fishing for Woolmer Green Angling Club. It has a large number of water fowl though recently it has been rather over-run by Canada geese. These seem to fly down the railway line and then branch off towards Mardleybury when they reach Woolmer Green.

Mardleybury Manor some time before it was rendered in the 1930s. In 1740, a toll-gate was erected on this road where it disappears out of sight in the picture. Additional sidegates for taking tolls on droves of cattle were allowed by Acts of 1763 and 1784.

Mardleybury Farmhouse from the front in 1913.

Mardleybury Farmhouse from the back in 1913.

The listed barn at Mardleybury Farm.

The old sign at Mardleybury Farm: 'Mardleybury herd of pedigree Herefords'.

ECHOES FROM THE LATE IRON AGE (100BC–AD50)

In October 1904 an amphora was found in a pit approximately 2.5m x 2m x 3m 'dug for the purpose', and with ashes spread on the bottom surface. Most of the amphora was salvaged for the Hertford Museum. Yet another has since been found and is in the possession of Mr Wallace of Swangley's Farm, the tenant of the gravel pit. This fourth amphora was given in due course to Hitchin Museum. A black pot apparently found inside the fourth amphora is in Stevenage Museum. Andrews gives the position: in a gravel pit in an arable field on Mardleybury land, high up on the hill at about 90m OD, a few yards north of the north section of the Welwyn Tunnel. The 1898 OS 25" plan shows a small field surrounded by woodland, south of the footpath mentioned by Andrews and which is now Turpins Chase. The site is built over.

A widespread late-Iron-Age site was discovered by Lockleys Archaeological Society during the laying of the gas pipe from Welwyn to Widford in 1968; this runs past the south side of the farmhouse SW to NE.

A number of pits and ditches possibly of an enclosure were recorded with much late-Iron-Age debris and a scatter of Roman pottery was found south-west of the farm; also to the south-west is a substantial bank and ditch, Perry's Grove earthwork, which may also date from the same period.

Perry's Grove bank and ditch are between 80 and 90 per cent complete and there is what may be a causeway across the ditch roughly in the middle. The site was accepted as a late pre-Roman, Iron-Age boundary although it is associated primarily with the late Iron Age. It may have functioned at a later date as a woodland boundary (Perry's Wood, on early county maps) and was part of the parish boundary.

Clearing the pond at Mardleybury in 1990.

Pedigree bull at Mardleybury.

HEMPSTALL SPINNEY: AN EARLY MEDIEVAL SITE (AD410–1066)

Hempstall Spinney is to be found west of Robbery Bottom Lane. In the Verulamium Museum at St Albans there is a Byzantine coin discovered by the roots of a tree during felling at Hempstall Spinney in the 1950s. The coin was identified as a follies of Justinian by Dr Kent, although he had his doubts as to whether or not it was a genuine find as it was unpatinated. As it turned out, the finder had carried it in his pocket for a number of years which had given the coin its shine.

The position of the find was just south of the Roman highway from St Albans to Braughing and Colchester, a road which was apparently still in use at this period; from a point just north-east of the spinney it still exists.

 Vera Mardlin with her horse outside the old barn at Mardleybury Farm.

✳ Alfred Barnes, Will Jackson, Lowie Wilsher and
Jean Sharpe with a Holstein Friesian cow, taken
during the First World War.

✳ A calf and a bull from
the Mardleybury herd.

✳ *Road workers in the 1920s. This group includes Mr Gregory, Mr Newman and Mr Burges. The men went round from village to village.*

Redlands & Carver's Croft

Carrying on towards Woolmer Green, the new estate of Carver's Croft was built in the 1990s on a large area of land which was owned by Wallace and Innes, gravel extractors who supplied gravel to many concerns, including Stevenage New Town. The site was eventually bought by Redlands, road contractors, who became one of the main employers in the village. One resident recalls that there was an early-morning workman's bus for the labourers working on road repairs.

The old Redlands site before Carver's Croft was built.

The site shortly after the fire.

Building in progress on Carver's Croft.

Woolmer Green's gardeners are justly proud of their work; this is Peter Webber's Holly Road garden.

The Four Roads on the South Side

Of the four roads on the left as you enter the village, the last three, Holly, Birch and Oak, were, together with Bridge Cottages (now Bridge Road), the first council houses built in Woolmer Green between the wars. Pam Norris, born in 1934, was the first baby born in any of these new roads.

Each road was planted with trees to reflect its name and a few of these trees still survive.

There are cropmarks of Roman origin (AD50–419) just behind the back of the last house on the left down Broadfield Road approximately 60 metres by 55 metres in size with an east-facing entrance. A linear ditch extends to the west of the enclosure. The position is on the brow of a hill, and the linear ditch runs into an area of marlpits.

Pam Norris with some of the evacuees on Mardley Heath. People were paid to take in evacuees in 1940, and Mrs Munnings who lived up Heath Road was the person who acted as the evacuees' officer. They came mainly from London and Eastbourne. Local children have good memories of the days when they shared their homes with the new children: 'Mum had a double bed and single bed downstairs in front room; we all slept upstairs. We had wonderful fights between the village children and the evacuees.' After the war the children were taken on days out to the seaside, mostly to Southend.

Standing on the path by the railway leading to Datchworth Green and looking down the hill towards Mardleybury Farm; Broadfield Road houses on the left, Datchworth in the distance.

The Old Village Hall

The old village hall was built after the First World War and was truly a community effort with 'villagers buying bricks for a penny each'. The two old foundation stones which are built into the new hall are engraved with inscriptions: 'Erected by the efforts of Mrs. Melchior, Tewin Old Rectory', and 'Stone laid by Viscount Knebworth 25 June 1930.' Indeed, the land had been given by Viscount Knebworth. The hall was leased from Mrs Melchior during her lifetime and on her death in 1959 became the property of Welwyn Parish Council; in 1965 it was valued at £200. During the Second World War, as recalled by one villager, 'Sainsburys took over the Village Hall as accommodation/canteen for people who were working at the depot.' There is still a covenant on the land which says that it should be used for educational purposes only. The hall was run by a voluntary committee and Betty Cray took all the bookings until it was knocked down.

 The WI put on a Pierrot show at the old Village Hall in the 1940s.

For the Christmas Play of 1976 the village children were dressed to represent different countries.

Queen Bee put on by the WI with Mrs O'Neill, Mrs Orton, Mrs Brownsell,
Mrs White, Mrs Hogan and Mrs Head.

The WI with Mrs Head, Mrs Hogan, Mrs Harvey, Mrs Orsham, Mrs Phillips, Mrs White, Mrs Jeffery, Mrs Chalkley,
Mrs Holm and Mrs Parker. Judging by the patriotic flag on the wall this must have been
coronation year, 1953.

The WI in the 1950s with Mrs O'Neill, Mrs Head, Mrs Hogan and Mrs Tetley.

A Norwegian Wedding put on by the WI with Mrs Brownsell, Mrs Bowyer, Mrs White, Mrs Orsman, Mrs Orton, Mrs Nutting and Mrs Harvey.

✷ *Fancy-dress night at the WI in the 1960s. Included are:*
Mrs Clements, Enid White, Mrs Dietrich, Mrs Brownsell,
Mrs Parker, Mrs Head, Mrs Jeffery, Mrs Chapman.

✷ *Evelyn and Dorothy Tucker were a Guide and a Brownie in 1940.*

Three members of ✷
the popular
village dance band:
'Tommy' Thompson, 'Blondie'
Cooke and Roy Arnold.

MEMORIES OF THE OLD HALL

'In the Village Hall they would have picture shows.
A man would come in his van, the projectionist, and set up.
They would sell balloons outside for the kiddies.
The children used to jump up and down to make shadows
on the screen and they would get quite rowdy. Sometimes
the film would break or the equipment break down and
everyone would be in uproar banging and shouting.'

'There were dances every Saturday and of course American GIs during the war.
Always chewing gum, they were camped over on the heath with all their lorries for a couple of months.
First time we ever saw bananas, which were willingly given by the servicemen.'

'Harold Edwards did a lot for the village, he ran a youth club twice a week and bingo once a week.
Once a month we had a dance with a band; these were all held in the Village Hall.'

'At the Queen's Silver Jubilee we had a show in the Village Hall. All the children had little candles and sang.
Mr and Mrs Gardner had arranged it all for the children – races, lunch and tea, and in the evening a dance.
The children were given a flag and certificate, a coin and a mug.'

'The Village Hall was cheap and cheerful, people felt they could use it. You would meet
people at mother and baby clinic, and that would continue on and you would then see them at school.
Activities for young people included Brownies, dancing, church choir and school choir.'

'Mrs Head of the WI put on concerts and shows in the old Village Hall.'

THE 1st WELWYN SCOUT GROUP meets at Scout Headquarters, Lockleys Drive, Welwyn, as follows:

    Mondays 6.30 to 7.45 p.m. Cub Scouts (8 to 11 years)
    Tuesdays 6.30 to 7.45 p.m. Cub Scouts
    Fridays 7.30 to 9.00 p.m. Scouts (11 to 16 years)

The Group Scout Leader is Mr. B. C. Archer, 111 Warren Way, Digswell. Leaders are urgently required to assist in this group of approximately 100 boys. Experience is not essential as training can be arranged.

The SECOND WELWYN GUIDE COMPANY and BROWNIES offer a warm welcome to girls wishing to join. They should apply to the Guide Captain, Miss D. Cordle, 4 Colyer Close, Welwyn (Tel: 5625). The meetings take place in the Evangelical Church Hall, Fulling Mill Lane, Welwyn, at the following times:

    Brownies: Mondays 5.30 to 7.00 p.m. (8 to 11 years)
    Guides: Fridays 6.15 to 7.45 p.m. (11 to 15 years)

The 1st WELWYN BROWNIE PACK meet at Scout Headquarters, Lockleys Drive, on Thursdays from 6.30 to 7.30 p.m. Enquiries can be made to Miss B. Scott, 27 Heathcote Avenue, Hatfield, or Mrs. Blamire-Brown, The Rectory, Tewin. Helpers are needed to assist with the Pack.

The 1st WOOLMER GREEN BROWNIES meet on Fridays at 5.30 p.m. in Woolmer Green School. Membership is for girls from 7 to 11 years who subscribe 3d per week. There are no vacancies at the moment but there will be some coming up regularly and enquiries should be made to the Brownie Guider, Mrs. S. Hoar, Police House, Woolmer Green (Tel: Knebworth 2222)

TREFOIL GUILD (Welwyn & Knebworth District); anyone over 18 who has been enrolled in the Guides can keep an interest in Guiding and help companies and Brownie packs by joining the Trefoil Guild. New members are always welcome and the subscription is 7/6d a year. Information from The Hon. Mrs. Dawson, 3 Copse Hill, Robbery Bottom Lane, Welwyn (Tel: 4745); Mrs. Dillis, Sherborne, Station Road, Digswell; Mrs. Cooper, 6 School Lane, Welwyn.

The First Woolmer Green Brownies and the Over 60 Club were both popular in 1970.

SIXTY PLUS

WELWYN JUBILEE OLD FOLKS' CLUB meets at 37 High Street, Welwyn, for the benefit of all people in Welwyn Rural District of pensionable age. The club provides a meeting place for social gatherings and entertainment, comradeship for the lonely and care for members when they are sick or otherwise housebound. Club afternoons are held every Monday and Thursday throughout the year. Enquiries to Mr. and Mrs. C. Simmons, Bridge House, High Street, Welwyn. (Tel: 4471).

MEETINGS OF WELWYN FRIENDSHIP (Over 60's) CLUB are held at the Civic Centre, Welwyn, every Monday (except Bank Holidays) at 2 p.m. The subscription is 4s per annum. Members must be residents of Welwyn, Digswell, The Ayots or Oaklands, and over 60 years of age. The Secretary is Mrs. E. F. Adams, 28 Mill Lane, Welwyn (Tel: 4574).

WOOLMER GREEN OVER 60 CLUB meets on Friday afternoons from 2.00 to 4.00 p.m. in the Club building at the rear of Woolmer Green Village Hall. There are vacancies for a few new members living in the locality, both men and women. The objects of the club are to provide companionship, entertainment, outings and mutual help. There is no entrance fee and the annual subscription is 4s 6d. A well patronised whist drive is held on the first Monday of each month (Bank Holidays excepted) at Woolmer Green Village Hall at 8.00 p.m. It is open to all. The President of the club is Mr. P. D. Sapsed, Mardley Bury Farm, Woolmer Green; Chairman, Mrs. Swinscow, Paynes Farm, New Road, Woolmer Green (Tel: Knebworth 3345); Secretary, Mrs. M. Fletcher, 2 Normans Lane, Rabley Heath, Welwyn (Tel: Knebworth 2193). The club is associated with the Herts. Old Peoples Welfare Council.

Woolmer Green Carpet Bowls Club with the winner's shield in 1978 in the old Village Hall.

The children who put on the show at the Queen's Silver Jubilee.

People were surprised when the hall was declared unsafe by Welwyn Parish Council as a lot of money had just been spent on it. Villagers were very upset when the breakers moved in in January 1991.

Brown Owl, Shirley Staniforth, was good at digging.

Brownies help at the old Village Hall site.

HERTFORDSHIRE

VILLAGE VENTURES
COMPETITION
1991/92

FOURTH PRIZE

PRESENTED TO

Woolmer Green Resident's Association

IN RECOGNITION OF ACTIVE INVOLVEMENT IN THE
PRESERVATION OF RURAL COMMUNITY LIFE IN HERTFORDSHIRE

Community Council for Hertfordshire   Shell U.K. Limited

July 3rd 1992
Date

THE JOLLY GARDEN

After the old Village Hall site had been left derelict for some time the Residents' Association decided to turn it into a garden and received an award from Village Ventures for their efforts, the certificate of which is shown *above*. They named it 'The Jolly Garden' after Brian Jolly, headmaster of the village school, who died suddenly in 1991.

Walking along New Road towards Paynes Farm in the 1950s.

Ann Swinscow and her daughter in 1968 with one of the foals at Paynes Farm.

Paynes Farm

Paynes Farm is the first house on the road from Datchworth to Woolmer Green. It is set in a sheltered landscape of rising chalk fields and lies at the junction of two lanes one of which has been lost. The first building at Paynes Farm was probably standing as far back as the sixteenth century and the original brick chimney still exists. There are two wells close to the house.

In Elizabethan times the building was two farm cottages, which probably belonged to Mardleybury Manor. When the last tenant farmed there it was part of the Knebworth Estate.

At the time of the Tithe Award in 1837 there were three buildings shown, with the present house lying roughly east to west, another building to the north of it and another structure to the south-west.

Looking up the road towards Datchworth from Paynes Farm.

Just before the house is reached there is a field called 'Saw Pit Field' which refers to the practice of sawing timber for building by the use of a pit dug into the ground. One sawyer would stand in the pit under the piece of wood whilst another would stand on the wood itself and they would each have the end of a long saw which would be drawn up and down into the pit cutting the wood into timbers.

At the time of the second Series Ordnance Survey map, 1884, the farm was referred to as 'Leggat's Farm'.

OWNERS AND OCCUPIERS

At the time of the Tithe Award the owner of the farm was William Blake, perhaps the same Blake who gave land for the school. The occupier was William Pain whose daughter became a schoolmistress in 1839 and served continuously until her retirement in 1874. She became the first mistress at Woolmer Green School in 1859 and before this she kept a 'Dame School' which was possibly held in a room at Paynes Farm or in the barn at Wren Cottage in New Road. Jane Pain was born in 1823 and died in 1911 at the age of 88; she was 14 when the Tithe Award was carried out in 1837 and established the Dame School in 1839 two years later when she was 16 years old.

The last people to farm the property were called Burgess when it belonged to the Knebworth Estate of the Lytton family and the children of local families were sent to buy milk from the farm, it being only about half its present size.

Around 1900 the Cottons of Gun Lodge (the Great North Road Hotel) took over the tenancy and did much to transform the building by adding a large extension to the front of the house and a further extension at the rear. They made the two acres of farmland into a very attractive garden.

After this a lady called Mrs Manningham-Buller rented the house. She was a relative of the Attorney General of the time and the house, having been improved by the Cottons, was at this time thought of as a dwelling of good status rather than a working farm.

Mrs F. Manningham-Buller was a keen gardener and was very proud of the herbaceous borders and the enormous variety of plants that she grew. She also worked as an artist specialising in flowers and is known to have exhibited her work at The Society of Women Artists a dozen times between 1917 and 1923, by which time her address was at Chester Street, London. Mrs Manningham-Buller changed the name of the house from Paynes Farm to Woolmer Green End.

When she died Lord and Lady Kilmarnock moved into the house, having been living at Homewood in Old Knebworth. When they left the house was sold to Mr and Mrs B.W.H. Scott. Mr Scott was an architect and together with his wife carried out considerable repairs to the building during their occupancy.

The subsequent owners of the house were Mr and Mrs Swinscow (he was a Parish Councillor) who established the famous 'Kirkstall Shetland Pony Stud' at the farm, bringing back an agricultural use to the property once more after a break of half a century. These ponies were shown widely. Mrs Swinscow was an artist before her marriage and painted the house and the gardens.

The end houses in New Road, from which point on it is open fields. ✴

✴ *Phyllis Smalley and Fred Archer during the war. At this time if you walked up to the top of Mardley Hill in the late evenings you could see London burning below.*

New Road, by Paynes Farmhouse, has ✴ *seen some bad floods. Located in a hollow between watersheds and with no path for a river to drain the water away has meant that Woolmer Green was a marshy area with many ponds, all, except the present village pond, now having been filled in. The water mainly soaks away into the underground aquifers which are now tapped for drinking water. Prior to this there were numerous wells around the village, possibly as many as 50.*

Garden Road & New Road

The terrace of three white houses was built for the employees of Kimpton's, the bakers. The pathway at the side links New Road with Mardleybury. The new houses on the right in Garden Road and Garden Close are mainly built on gardens or allotments which were carefully tended by villagers. There was also a paddock here and Salisbury's woodyard was sited in Garden Road. The equipment on the small children's playground was erected after the war.

The Fox

The first record of a building on the site of The Fox at Woolmer Green dates from the nineteenth century and describes a cottage built by William Warren 'on a piece of waste ground lying within the manor of Mardleybury at Woolmer Green in the Parish of Welwyn'. It appears to have been used as a beerhouse since 1844 with a blacksmith's shop and general store attached. At one time it also included a bakehouse. Joseph Haggar was recorded as its first keeper in 1871. He was a local man, who also worked as a farm labourer like many other publicans and beerhouse keepers of the time. His wife, Mary, came from Welwyn and, at the time when he ran The Fox, they had two children, Newman and Katherine.

There were also boarders living at The Fox then – Benjamin Holton and George Wrens, both of whom were farm labourers. At this time there was a shop attached.

Benjamin Young of Hertford, brewers, had an interest in the pub in 1860. Many agricultural labourers lived in the vicinity of The Fox in the 1870s as well as two boot and shoe makers, a chandler, shopkeeper and a hurdle maker. There were also several railway plate-layers, station staff and signalmen in the village.

The Fox is now owned by McMullens. Before it was done up after the Second World War the right-hand side was still a separate cottage which was lived in by the woodcarver, Harry Macdonald, when he arrived in the village. Doris Tyler and her husband Bill were the tenants at The Fox for many years. Coming out to Woolmer Green from London they loved their time at the pub and the friendliness of all the villagers. There are a number of stories connected with the pub, one being that Dick Turpin and his highwaymen lived in Mardleybury woods nearby. The Fox was also known as a den of thieves.

It is a tradition that Morris dancers perform here on the May bank holiday. The barn at Wren Cottage can be seen in the top picture.

The Fox in the early 1900s.

The Fox, soon after it was renovated.

BEST GARDENS
There has been a cup awarded over the last few years for the Best Garden which subsequently was changed to The Best Front Garden. The awards ceremony was held at The Fox.

Clockwise from top: Peter Long, Woolmer Green Councillor with the old Rural District Council, and his wife at the award ceremony for the Best Garden Competition in The Fox in 1992; Betty Clements with her certificate; Mrs Dearman with her certificate; Peter Webber with the cup. The rules had to be changed after he kept winning it year after year!

23 New Road   Helen.R.

The house I wrote to was opposite Mrs Mardian's house. My house has common bonding common bonding looks like this.

My house has a wooden ponch. My house is terraced. There front garden looks as thogh she shares it with next door. The out side of it there is a wall about 1 mere high.

She has a chimney with four pipes. I have knot got much information because I did knot kescue a letter. this is my house.

Gary Drury is standing in the doorway.

25 NEW ROAD
Three former farmworkers' cottages are on the left just after the footpath to Mardleybury. When Tuse Drury moved into the middle one in 1959 they were completely unimproved. These evocative pictures show No.25 when the Drurys rented it from Mr Wallace for 16s.0d. a week.

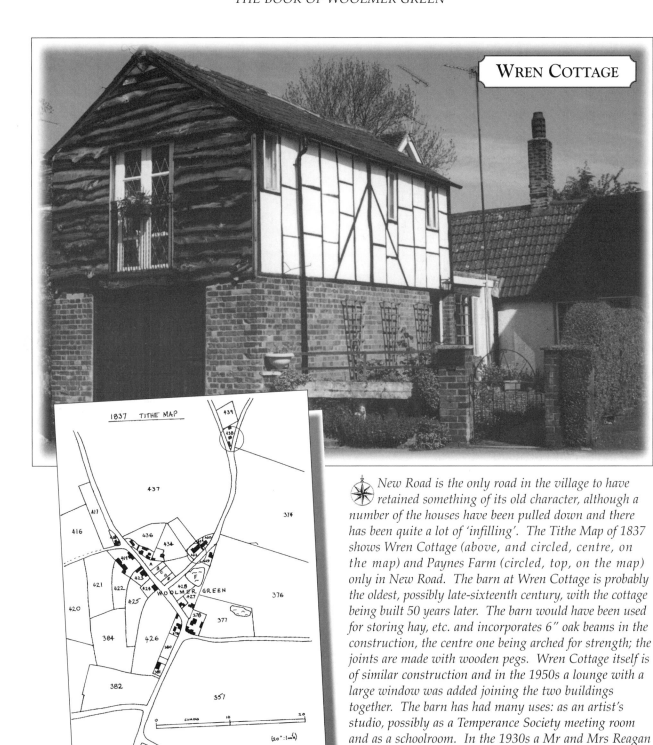

WREN COTTAGE

1837 TITHE MAP

New Road is the only road in the village to have retained something of its old character, although a number of the houses have been pulled down and there has been quite a lot of 'infilling'. The Tithe Map of 1837 shows Wren Cottage (above, and circled, centre, on the map) and Paynes Farm (circled, top, on the map) only in New Road. The barn at Wren Cottage is probably the oldest, possibly late-sixteenth century, with the cottage being built 50 years later. The barn would have been used for storing hay, etc. and incorporates 6" oak beams in the construction, the centre one being arched for strength; the joints are made with wooden pegs. Wren Cottage itself is of similar construction and in the 1950s a lounge with a large window was added joining the two buildings together. The barn has had many uses: as an artist's studio, possibly as a Temperance Society meeting room and as a schoolroom. In the 1930s a Mr and Mrs Reagan lived in the cottage and set up a dancing school in the barn, hauling a grand piano up through the big doors.

It could possibly have been in the barn at Wren Cottage that Woolmer Green had a coffee club. These are the coffee-room accounts for 1898 to 1899.

ACCOUNTS OF COFFEE ROOM AT WOOLMER GREEN
1898-1899.

RECEIPTS.	£	s.	d.	EXPENDITURE.	£	s.	d.
Members' Subscriptions	1	5	1	Caretaker, Coal, and Oil ..	1	3	0
Hon. Members	1	10	0	Lamp....................	0	6	9
Mothers' Meeting	0	5	0	Chairs	0	15	0
Balance due	0	11	10	Table...................	1	1	0
				Rent	0	6	6
	£3	11	10		£3	11	11

✴ *Ash Cottage in New Road. An article in the Hertfordshire Countryside tells how:*

John King had his workshop in New Road: 'one cannot miss either the house or the workshop because it is the only house in New Road which is sideways on to the road. John King served the village well, both as a shoemaker and a councillor. On Sunday, he would be transformed, for he donned a top hat, a frock coat, gloves, spats and, with a gay twirl of his stick, set off for the long walk to Welwyn, for John King was a preacher at the nonconformist chapel in that village.'

✴ *All the old houses in the village had outside wash-houses and toilets like this one at the rear of Mark Wilde's house in New Road. Main drainage came quite late to Woolmer Green; some of these drains have just had to be replaced. The growth in the population meant that the original main drainage pipes could not cope. On several occasions the man-hole cover at 9 New Road used to blow which meant that Chris and Rosemary Cooper had to wade through feet of sewage to reach their house!*

Mr Cecil Tucker won this cup for the best vegetables in the 1940s.
Inset: One of the houses opposite The Fox (where Tuse's father lived) which had
such lovely front gardens.

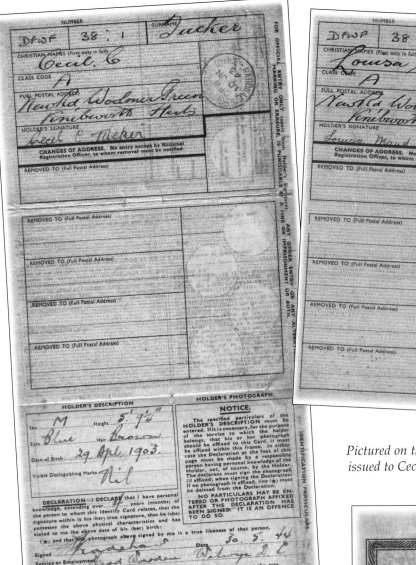

Pictured on this page are the identity cards issued to Cecil and Louisa Tucker in 1943.

WAR YEARS

During the Second World War, Mr Tucker was an air-raid warden, as was Harry Macdonald. One of the duties of the Home Guard was to mount patrols at the railway tunnels in case any parachutists came down. A local resident recalls:

Woolmer Green dads built a deep air-raid shelter at the back of the school. There was not much headroom so the staff sat on the top! We did sometimes get daytime alerts, not only could you see crosses on wings but features of crews. There was quite a bit of reconnaissance as there were armaments made in local factories.

Most of the women were employed during the war, in the Sainsbury's depot, for example, or they took in refugees, crowding them into their small homes. A lady who lived in Heath Road was the officer who housed them. People have fond memories of the war years, of cycling round the nearly empty roads and of exploring the glorious countryside in those hot summers.

15 New Road

I went to Mrs Chalkley to find some History. I wrote to Mrs Chalkley who lives at number 15 down New Road, she has lived in her house 62 years but I don't now how old the actuall house is.

When Mrs Chalkley first came here there were a bakers red lion farm yard and cheauers inn. The cheauers inn was on the road. They took that down and built a new one in its place.

Harry Macdonald was very famous and he died in 1964 he was famous for making carvings out of wood he mostly carved dogs when he was alive he used to charge people to come and look at his carvins. Mrs Chalkley lived Just up the Road to Harry.

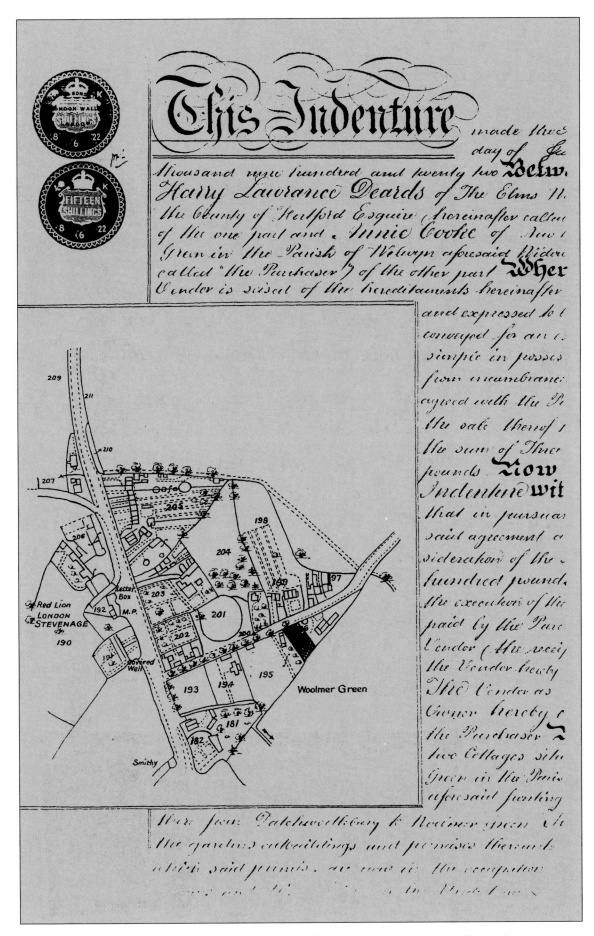

Indenture for the sale of 15 New Road in 1922. The plan is of much earlier origin.

8 New Road

I can tell the house I
wrote to is old because I
can tell by the window frames
The house is up New Road No8
The house has a green door.
The owner has built an
arch above the front door
The roof tiles are a blueish
grey colour. The roof tiles
are made from slate. It
is a terrace house. It is
a small house. The house

I wrote to is on a map which was printed in 1972
Which makes it 17 years old. It has a sill at the
bottom of the house. A sill is used for decoration.

Vena Britten (later Evans) and her brother Ron with their parents, Charlie and Ethel during the First World War. Ethel recalled: 'My mother looks very cross because father had to be fetched from the pub when the photographer arrived. There was a tap over the road from the cottage and when I was little there was the Black Pond over the road where the overflow water from the pond used to accumulate and people would throw all their rubbish there. I wasn't allowed to go down there.'

Looking across the pond to No.6 New Road.

 The pond in the 1970s with the swan called George. This was before Vera Mardlin arranged for the bank to be built up at the side of the road.

WOOLMER GREEN POND

The pond is thought to have given Woolmer Green its name being the mere at which wolves drank: Wolversmere which became Woolmer.

The pond is one of Woolmer Green's main assets, having been used throughout the ages for watering both man and beast, and carts would be driven into the pond to swell the wood of their wheels so that the metal tyres stayed firmly in place.

The following is just a handful of memories about the pond:

'I remember my grandfather clearing the silt from the pond in the 1920s. He had a cart with a plank behind it which he dragged along the bottom...'

'There weren't many ducks when I was young, we used to catch them and eat them!'

'We used to skate round the pond in the winter – it was magical.'

The community get together to restore the pond, 1983.
The reeds were very, very heavy.

✦ *The float is pulled over the pond during island building.*

✦ *Helpers including Vera Mardlin, Steve Catlin and Sue Graves, 1983.*

It looks like fun but it's a mucky job. The children used to get back home at night completely exhausted and smelling terrible; there were more hot baths run that year than ever before! ✦

Woolmer Green Pond

In 1975 Mrs Mardlin wrote to the Save the Village Pond Campaign which was run by the *Daily Telegraph* to ask for their help in building up the bank to the pond which stood alongside the road. Mr Kidner wrote to Welwyn Parish Council and eventually it was decided to rebuild the bank. At the same time concrete bollards were put at intervals along the roadside to prevent parking alongside the pond which tended to break the bank down.

The sum of £25 was collected from people in the village to buy turf as the Council would not pay for this. This was laid by Mr Nicolson and Mrs Mardlin. With some of Mrs Mardlin's daffodils and a little more money which was collected it was possible to plant daffodils around each of the bollards to make them appear less obtrusive in the spring.

It was not until 1983 and the summer holidays that Mrs Mardlin wondered if, with children and some mums, they could cut back the reeds which have lovely yellow flowers and look pretty in early summer. She wrote to the Parish Council to ask for their help in providing a trailer to take away the reeds and a working party of schoolchildren and mums was organised. Mr Geary made a wooden float which had a RAF air bag on it to help it float better. Another float was also made up with about 18 gallon washing-up liquid containers and a fork-lift pallet. Each child worked hard and then had a float on the pallet, a drink of orange and sweets which one or two kind ladies gave. It took two days to chop back the reeds approximately a metre and a half wide with axes and choppers. Not only were the reeds extremely heavy but they floated off across the pond and looked very messy. Eventually they were manhandled to one side and allowed to dry off before being lifted away. The reeds were nearly a metre long with big tubers on them which went deep into the mud, and they also had big seed pods on them which dried up from the flowers.

In all, four trailers were filled, each one being taken away by the Council at the end of the day and another one delivered ready for the next morning. The *Welwyn Times* came and took photographs, one with all the children piled up on top of the reeds on the trailer. Everyone was very dirty, covered in black sludge from the pond bottom. You have never seen so many dirty children and grown-ups!

Later that holiday it was decided to build an island to encourage larger birds to nest at the pond. Stones and rocks from all over the village were collected.

The Canada geese go walkabout and get as far as The Fox.

Mrs Nicolson helped to push wheelbarrow loads back to the pond which were manoeuvred out using the floats, several children loading each one. Then with a rope on either end of the float Mrs Geary walked out and sunk the first rocks in the middle. Each day someone went out to take a turn unloading the rocks on the island and sent the float back to the helpers standing on dry land. In this way the float did not get away too many times although it frequently tipped over losing all the rocks.

To get soil out to the island was another problem which was solved with the aid of several chaff bags joined together. Trevor Lowndes had a heap of topsoil which he kindly donated, and a group set to and filled up the bags and tied them up with bale string. Then with another float made from an inflatable dinghy with a large board laid on top the group floated out the 30 newly-made bags putting them around the outside to form a firmer edge. Any odd pieces of turf from people's gardens were also added. Then heavy rain came, the holidays were over and the island was just visible all winter.

In 1984 during the summer holidays the floats and the children came out again and another layer was built up on the island with the whole lot being topped off with more turf which of course the ducks loved to eat.

By 1996 the pond was still silting up very badly and each year saw an increase in the algae growth. There was very little water in the pond by this point and each summer the pond dried up causing people to try to provide water for the ducks by digging holes and filling them with water using hoses from their houses!

A village meeting was called to discuss what should be done and it was decided to dredge the pond properly with the help of the Countryside Management team from the County Council. There was much debate over whether this should be done at all and whether the pond would ever hold water again but things were becoming so serious that drastic action had to be taken. Finding somewhere for the water to go was very difficult – it was always the 'wrong sort of water'! The silt was taken by road to Cave Wood where permission had been obtained for it to be dumped in a big hole in the ground. It took a long time for the rain to arrive that year but it did come and finally there was a formal opening of the pond which was a great success.

 The slurry tanker took the surface water away.

The silt was very deep and very smelly.

 Pumping the water out of the pond prior to beginning the dredging.

Up to 4ft of silt was dredged out of the pond.

Andy Hardstaff from Countryside Management nearly got stuck in the mud.

Geoff Cox and Tony Catlin doubt that the pond will ever be the same again.

The silt being loaded into a truck.

141

✴ A pair of Canada geese has nested on the island ✴ at the pond on a regular basis for a number of years. When the goslings hatch the parent geese walk them along the path to Mardleybury Pond where there is a colony of Canada geese. Here, once getting as far as The Fox, they then decide to hurry back home again.

New Road, by the pond, used to flood ✴ very badly. ✴

✴ Soon after the pond was cleared there ✴ was a bad infestation of blanket weed and it was very hard work to remove it. Sam Wilson is pictured here tackling the task. Nigel Jolly is deep in the water.

✳ *Opening Day and the pond clearance is complete, 1997.*

Andy Hardstaff from Countryside Management ✳
cut the ribbon. Behind him is Dorothy Jackson.

✳ *Children clap as the ribbon is cut.*

The Iced Diamond Jazz Band played at the ✳
opening ceremony.

HOW WE CAN LOOK AFTER OUR POND

Limit the amount of bread given to the water fowl, throwing it on the bank and not in the water so that other birds can eat any surplus.

Always refer any ideas about the pond to the Pond Committee whose names are on the Parish Notice Board.

With everyone's co-operation, the pond will be conserved in its natural habitat.

Looking over the pond towards No.2 New Road in the 1970s. The yellow flag irises that surround the pond always draw admiring comments. The roof of the Post Office can be seen in the background.

2 NEW ROAD

The Misses Cross lived at No.2 New Road. Their father, who was the station-master at Knebworth and also a churchwarden just after the church was built, had bought quite a lot of the old cottages in the village which were rented out and gradually sold off during their lifetime. They had an orchard across the road where New Court is today.

One of the sisters is well remembered because she 'wore very mannish clothes, plus fours and a deer-stalker hat. She would chase children away from the grass in front of her house.' Another local recalls scrumping apples from the Misses Cross' orchard.

Ron Britten contributed this vibrant memory:

Miss Cross said that when she died I could have the furniture in her house, but when I got there I picked up the only chair and it fell to pieces in my hands: it was riddled with woodworm.

Ann and Joan loved their garden at No.5 New Road.

Called 'Claude' by some and 'Maurice' by others, this Muscovy was a real village character.

A lovely garden in New Road belonging to Sheila and Roy Rogers, c.1994.

Looking at 3 New Road from the side of the pond.

145

Billy Pedder at the side of his house, No.3 New Road.

These houses are now known as 3 and 5 New Road. No.3 was certainly two cottages at one time, if not three. The back part of the single-storey building is now No.5 New Road; it is one of the oldest buildings in the village.

The old lean-to greenhouse at the side of No.3 New Road. This house was once a shop and the 'vinegar flats' sold to the children are fondly remembered. At one time it was an alehouse where beer was sold to villagers.

A view of the pond in the early 1900s.

These cottages by the pond date from the nineteenth century. The row of three cottages by the pond seems much the same as it has always been. The chimneys were re-built during the 1980s to the same design as the originals, except that the corners are square instead of rounded.

Residents of New Road on Coronation Day, 1953.
Left to right, back row: Will Clements ('Duchy', in shorts), Charles Young (fancy shirt), Tinny Tucker, Ken Sisseman,
?, Gilbert Monk (with glasses), ?, Cecil Tucker (dark hair), Jack Webber (open shirt and jacket), ?,
'Red' (American serviceman, became Josie Clements' husband);
3rd row: Marta Fletcher (with stick), Elsie Monk (patterned dress), Peggy Sisseman, Evelyn Jackson (striped dress),
Mrs Tucker, Mrs Parker, Mrs Britten (dark dress), Vena Britten, Phil Jackson (with bushy hair), Evelyn Tucker (with
baby), Mrs D. Tucker (arms folded), Margaret Webber with baby John, Miss Corp (white dress, dark belt),
Tuse Tucker, Josie Clements (with bag);
2nd row: Gilly Evans, David Parker, Betty Clements (with cardigan), Ron Tucker (with tie),
Vi Tyler (dress with belt, black bow), Mrs Charles Young (was Peggy Moss), Carol Harrison (kneeling with bows),
Peter Webber (dark trousers), Mrs Young (sitting), Walter Fletcher (with stick);
children: ?, Susan Harrison, ?, ?, Carol Clements, ?, Yvonne Sisseman, ?, ?, Mary Evans, ?, Billy Tyler, ?, ?.

The coronation parties in 1953 were by street only rather than the whole village. New Road had their party in the
school. These two photographs show the New Road people enjoying the coronation celebration.
Above left: New Road children's tea showing Mrs Young, Evelyn Morris,
Peggy Sisseman and Yvonne Sisseman.
Above right: The children thought the cakes were wonderful.
Included in this picture are Linda Morris and Billy Tyler.

Left to right at the coronation tea: Vi Tyler, Evelyn Jackson, Mrs Corp, Tuse Tucker, Josie Clements, Vena Evans and Bill Fletcher.

New Road children's tea showing Mrs Britten, Elsie Monk, Ron Tucker, Mrs Young and Carol Harrison.

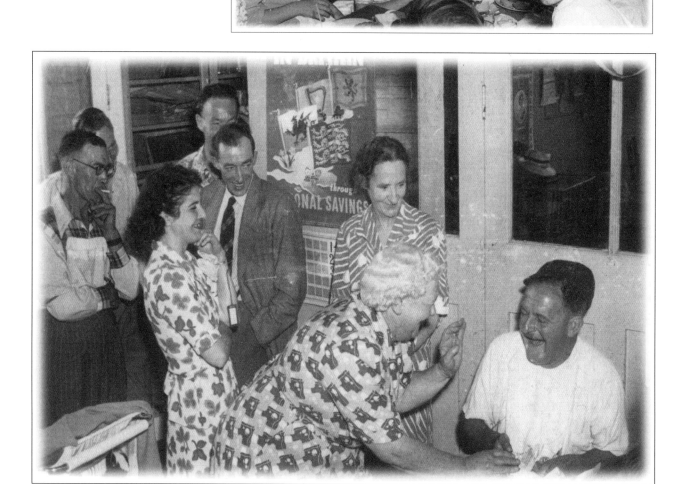

The photograph includes: Gilbert Monk, Charlie Young, Mr Tucker, Peggy Young, Mrs Young, Lou Tucker and Dutchy Clements.

Cutting the celebratory cakes at the coronation tea in 1953.

Left to right: Lou Tucker, Charlie Young, Evelyn Morris, Elsie Monck and Peggy Sisseman.

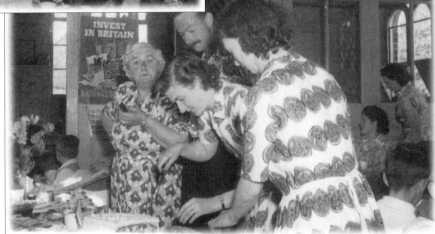

New Road coronation tea.

Races on Coronation Day. The picture includes, from left to right: Phyllis Jackson (who lived in the cottage at the side of The Fox), Dutchy Clements, Carol Clements, Cecil Tucker and Red Krantzler.

All of the New Road children at the coronation tea including Dutchy Clements who dressed up as a child!

And Now...

And now... What of the future? It goes without saying that it is just a bit more difficult to see what the future holds for us than it is to look back on the past. There are no photographs of the future, no records to unearth; but we can in some way shape our future whereas we have no control over our past.

In the last ten years Woolmer Green has seen its population nearly double. Although the latest census statistics are not yet to hand, we can fairly accurately say that our population is now over 1500, most of the increase being housed in the two new estates of Carver's Croft and Twin Foxes.

More than half of the houses and flats on these estates are starter homes and as such have a large turnover of occupants, which mitigates against a commitment to village life. However, it is nice to hear people say: 'We're looking for somewhere bigger in the village so we can stay.'

The terraces of old cottages, particularly along London Road and to some extent along New Road, have been combined to form larger dwellings resulting in people becoming more isolated from their neighbours. Although the houses some 50 or so years ago were often very basic compared with our modern needs, people lived more closely together and were more of a community. The demise of the village shops is very sad... perhaps we are partly to blame for not using them more.

The land behind The Fox has already been designated for new housing and we wonder which will be the next piece of land to go the same way. Green Belt land, as we know from the furore over the expansion to the west of Stevenage, is not sacrosanct.

The future lies with us and with the next generation. Now that we are the Parish of Woolmer Green we have more of an opportunity to shape it as we want. The Village Hall is now being used much more than it has been over the last ten years; our first Village Day was a great success: next year's could be even better! It's up to us – Woolmer Green is a wonderful place to live and now we can all have a say in what the future holds for us.

A sad sight! The Post Office Shop was taken over by an antiques firm for a time but is now empty.

A POEM BY CAROL COX, 1996

Woolmer Green is a wonderful place
You always see a friendly face
People stop and say hello!
When they're walking to and fro.

Mauvie and Vi in the paper shop
Sue and Co 'up the top'
All ready to serve with a friendly smile
And always ready to chat a while.

In the Spring the woods are a delight
The bluebells with their heads so bright
And if you're quiet when in here
You can even see a Muntjac deer.

Badger setts are all around
Rabbits and hare also abound
And if you're lucky, just like me
A wily fox you could even see.

If ever I have to move away
It might just happen, you know, one day
I'll not forget this Woolmer Green
And all the pleasure there has been.

The playground next to the village hall attracts young families from all around the area.

Carver's Croft is looking good now the trees are maturing but the houses change hands frequently.

What does the future hold for these young people seen at the Garden Road playground?

*One of the oldest inhabitants at
94, Sheila (Sally) Scott.*

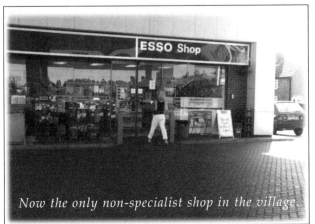

Now the only non-specialist shop in the village.

Land behind The Fox designated for housing.

A BALLAD OF WOOLMER GREEN
by Frank E. Ballin, September, 1969

In our old village, Woolmer Green's its name,
We have no claim to national mark or fame.
Throughout the ages undisturb'd it lay,
And this is still the case, we're pleased to say.
We trust its peace and quiet will long remain,
Though the North Road divides our vill in twain.

The swan-neck'd Edith, ere the Normans came
O'er Mardleybury and its wide domain
Held sway and in well-nigh a thousand years
Of divers lords the impress of each one bears.

Bartholomew of Badlesmere dwelt here
And did with Lancaster in arms appear
Until at Boroughbridge they vanquish'd were
And treason's direst penalties did bear.

Two hundred years elapsed and then held sway
Bluff King Hal with many a bloody day.
The luckless Gertrude saw her husband ta'en
To Tower Hill and there as traitor slain.

Poltergeists and phantoms do occur
As sundry local folk do well aver.
But when, as now, a scion of Godwin's line
Comes there to dwell, there is no further sign
Of ghoulies, ghosts and supernatural smell
That comes not forth from heaven or from hell.

An erstwhile farm lies on the Datchworth road,
There village worthies long made their abode.
The first school-marm of Woolmer Green dwelt there
And now once more her honoured name doth bear.

Against the church the former Cottage stands,
This house hath ever been in worthy hands
There three churchwardens in succession dwelt
Who've made their name in Woolmer Green long felt.

A Yorkshireman, Macdonald, came this way;
He liked the place full well and so did stay.
His model village you must not fail to view,
For 'tis far-fam'd from Cathay to Peru.

Of our old village we doubtless all do know
Much more. My muse now crieth Halt and so
We now must end the little résumé:
Good Luck to Woolmer Green now let us say.

Subscribers

Enid Aitchison, Bridge Road, Woolmer Green, Herts.

Alex and Rachel Akers, Woolmer Green

Sharon, Will, Chlöe and Emma Allanson, Woolmer Green, Herts.

Mr Steve Ansell, Scissett, West Yorkshire

Terry Archer, Panshanger

Anthony R. Armstrong, The Drive, Welwyn

Mr and Mrs S. Axon, Woolmer Green, Herts.

A. C. Barry

K. A. Barry, Hitchin, Herts.

Harding/Bazalgette family, Woolmer Green, Herts.

Peter, Gina, Simon and Hilary Beck, Woolmer Green, Herts.

Deborah Hewat and Michael Bennett, Eildon Cottage, Woolmer Green, Hert

Peter and Isabelle Best, Woolmer Green, Herts.

Luke and Georgina Bickers, Woolmer Green, Herts.

Nicola and Bill Bootle, Evergreen Lodge, Woolmer Green, Herts.

Mrs Evelyn Bowyer (née Deards), New York, USA

Mr R. Britten, Woolmer Green, Herts.

T. S. Brown, Digswell, Herts.

Mrs P. Brown, Woolmer Green, Herts.

David W. Brownsell, Woolmer Green, Herts.

Miss M. A. Bryant, Woolmer Green, Herts.

Richard J. Busby, Welwyn Garden City, Herts.

Stephen P. Cade, Twin Foxes, Woolmer Green, Herts.

M. R. and M. B. Cater, Woolmer Green, Herts.

His Honour Judge Brian Catlin, Woodcote, Oxon

Steven M. Catlin, Woolmer Green, Herts.

Joyce and Tony Catlin, Woolmer Green, Herts.

Danielle and Christina Chib,

Ian Chipperfield, Woolmer Green, Herts.

The Cloona family, Heath Road, Woolmer Green, Herts.

Codicote Local History Society

Geraldine Coleman, Woolmer Green, Herts.

Nick and Diana Collingridge, Woolmer Green, Herts.

Daniel Cooke, Digswell Park, Hertfordshire

Mr A. R. Cox, Country Properties, Knebworth, Herts.

Geoffrey and Susan Dash, Woolmer Green

Cis Davis, Woolmer Green, Herts.

Stephen, Marie, Iain and James Day, Broadfield Road, Woolmer Green, Herts.

Eddie and Val Deards, Woolmer Green, Herts.

Joan and Doug Dietrich

Timothy J. Dix, Woolmer Green, Herts.

Dorothy Drury (née Tuse Tucker), Woolmer Green, Herts.

Steve, Denise, Glenn and Suzanne Eldridge, New Road, Woolmer Green, Herts.

Bernard H. English

Mrs Vena Evans, Woolmer Green, Herts.

Enid Fairhead, Woolmer Green, Herts.

Nicholas Fenge, Woolmer Green, Herts.

Linda and Rick Fenge, Woolmer Green, Herts.

Georgina Fenge, Woolmer Green, Herts.

The Fleets', London Road, Woolmer Green, Herts.

Robert and Joan Fletcher, Woolmer Green, Herts.

Martine and David Game, Woolmer Green, Herts.

Sean Giddens, Bragbury End, Herts.

B. C. Goldsmith, Canberra ACT

L. F. Goldsmith, Camberra ACT
E. A. Golsmith, Woolmer Green, Herts.
Mrs Rosanna Goodson (née Roberts), Broadfield Road/now Welwyn Garden City
James Graves, Woolmer Green, Herts.
Richard S. Green, Woolmer Green, Herts.
Frances M. Green, Woolmer Green, Herts.
Mr and Mrs Keith Gregory, Longmead, Woolmer Green, Herts.
Peggy A. Gregory, Mardley Hill, Welwyn, Herts.
Mr and Mrs S. S. Grewal, Mayshade House, Woolmer Green, Herts.
Ms Leela K. Grewal, Mayshade House, Woolmer Green, Herts.
David, Meryl, Richard and Philip Hanlon, Holly House, Welwyn
Ali and Clive Harris, Woolmer Green, Herts.
Mrs Rosemary M. Hartley, Knebworth
Mr Darren John Hazard, Wickfield, Woolmer Green, Herts.
Jill A. Hewitt, Knebworth, Herts.
Jean Howarth (née Ingle), Broadstairs, Kent
Phyllis B. Jackson, Woolmer Green, Herts.
Mrs Linda Jacquet, Woolmer Green, Herts.
Nigel Jolly
Christina Jolly, Woolmer Green
Martyn Jolly
Dr Geoff Lawrence, Arches, Knebworth, Herts.
Frank Mac Mahon, Woolmer Green, Herts.
Mrs D. Mackay, Woolmer Green, Herts.
Mr and Mrs N. K. Maddex, Codicote, Herts.
Alan and Janis Manley, Woolmer Green, Herts.
Ian Marchbank and Ann Bruce, Woolmer Green, Herts.
Vera Mardlin, Ren Cottage, Woolmer Green, Hertfordshire
The McBroom family, Woolmer Green
Neil McDonald, Woolmer Green, Herts.
Mr S. J. Mizon, Woolmer Green, Herts.
Mrs E. J. Moody, Woolmer Green, Herts.
Lyn Morris (née Tucker), Devon/born Woolmer Green
Roland Moss, Oaklands, Welwyn, Herts.
Helen C. Neal, Cambridge
Joy Nicolson, Woolmer Green, Herts.
Mandy Norris, Woolmer Green, Herts.
Reg and Pam Norris, Woolmer Green, Herts.
Treena Norris, Woolmer Green, Herts.
Mr D. Nutting, Woolmer Green, Herts.

Mrs Eileen M. Orton, Woolmer Green, Herts.
Mr and Mrs D. Overman, Woolmer Green, Herts.
Mrs Ann Overton (née Deards), Bulls Green, Herts.
Mr and Mrs L. Pearce, Woolmer Green, Herts.
Sandra Pool, Woolmer Green, Herts.
S. and I. Porter, Woolmer Green, Herts.
Postman Peter
Eda and Ron Randles, Woolmer Green, Herts.
Andrew D. Rawnsley, Woolmer Green, Herts.
Susan Read, Woolmer Green, Herts.
Lorraine Recci, Welwyn Garden City, Herts.
Deborah and Farooq Rehmat, Woolmer Green, Herts.
Mr Adrian P. Roberts, Woolmer Green
Barbara J. Salisbury, Woolmer Green, Herts.
Don and Joy Sandford (née Jeffery), Welwyn Garden City
Delia Scott, Woolmer Green, Herts.
Mrs Sally Scott, Woolmer Green, Herts.
Sam Shaw, Woolmer Green, Herts.
Kenneth J. Sisseman, Woolmer Green, Herts.
Janet and Rob Slater, Mardley Hill, Herts.
Mr and Mrs R. Smalley, Woolmer Green, Herts.
Ann Sparks, Leigh-on-Sea, Essex
Mrs Ann Sparks, Leigh-on-Sea, Essex
St Michael's Woolmer Green Primary School
Kevin and Debbie Stammers, Woolmer Green, Herts.
Mrs S. Staniforth, Woolmer Green, Herts.
David and Jane Thom, Woolmer Green, Herts.
Ian and Frances Trevor, Woolmer Green, Herts.
Miss M. Tucker, Woolmer Green, Herts.
D. M. Tyler, Woolmer Green
Russell and Linda Vincent and family, Woolmer Green, Herts.
Geoffrey Wakefield, Hatfield
Mrs V. Wakefield
John Wallace, Watton-At-Stone, Herts.
John F. W. Walling, Newton Abbot, Devon
Judith Watson, Woolmer Green, Herts.
C. L. Watts and family
Jack A. Webber, Woolmer Green, Herts.
Peter Webber, Woolmer Green, Herts.
Jack Wood
Karen, Tom and Chlöe Wornham, Garden Road, Woolmer Green, Herts.

ALSO AVAILABLE IN THE SERIES

SOME OF THE MANY FORTHCOMING TITLES

The Book of Addiscombe, Vol. II • Various
The Book of Barnstaple • Avril Stone
The Book of Bridestowe • R. Cann
The Book of Buckland Monochorum • Pauline Hemery
The Book of Carshalton • Stella Wilks
The Book of Chagford • Ian Rice
The Book of Chittlehamholt with
Warkleigh & Satterleigh • Richard Lethbridge
The Book of Colney Heath • Bryan Lilley
The Book of Culmstock • Robert Garrett
The Book of Down St Mary • Various
The Book of Dulverton
with Brushford, Bury & Exebridge • Various
The Book of Dunster • Hilary Binding
The Book of Exmouth • W.H. Pascoe
The Book of Leigh and Bransford • Various
The Book of Lulworth • Rodney Legg
The Book of Markyate • Richard Hogg
The Book of Mawnan Smith • Various
The Book of Nether Stowey • Various
The Book of Newdigate • John Callcut
The Book of Newton Abbot • Ian Rice
The Book of North Tawton • Various
The Book of Northlew with Ashbury • Various
The Book of Okehampton • Radford & Radford
The Book of Peter Tavy • Various
The Book of Publow with Pensford • Various
The Book of Sampford Courtenay
with Honeychurch • Stephanie Pouya
The Book of Staverton • Pete Lavis
The Book of Studland • Rodney Legg
The Book of Wythall • Val Lewis

For details of any of the above titles or if you are interested in writing your own community history, please contact: Community Histories Editor, Halsgrove House, Lower Moor Way, Tiverton Business Park, Tiverton, Devon EX16 6SS, England, e-mail: sales@halsgrove.com

In order to include as many historic photographs as possible in this volume, a printed index is not included. However, the Community History Series is currently being indexed by Genuki. For further information and indexes to volumes in the series, please visit:

http://www.cs.ncl.ac.uk/genuki/DEV/indexingproject.html